Prophesy and Heal the Sick: How to Grow in Prophecy, Words of Knowledge, Healing, and Power Evangelism.

Matthew Helland

Prophesy and Heal the Sick

ISBN: 978-1-63302-077-1

Printed in the United States of America

Endorsements

"As you read this book, you will be inspired, informed, and I believe there will be an impartation that will take place as well. This is a must-read book for living out the fullness of the Spirit in our generation."
-Dr. A.D. Beacham, Jr., Bishop I.P.H.C. www.iphc.org

"During worship at a conference, Matt gave me a message from God about my past, my present and my future. This was both poignant and inspirational because it seemed to me that he knew everything about me even though we had never talked before. This deeply impacted me and I have been experiencing the positive effects of his words ever since. You are now holding his book in your hands. Be prepared that his words may change your life as well!"
-Attila Foris, Pastor at Autonomous Church and Leader of KIT Light Youth Movement, Budapest, Hungary, www.bpa.hu and www.kitinfo.hu

"During Matt Helland's School of Prophecy, I was released from all of my fears, resistance, and discomfort from all previous experiences I had regarding prophecy. What he says remains in line with what Jesus says, and what he does remains in line with love. He says that prophecy is all about Jesus and love. A striking summary of the difference that his teaching has made in my church: more of Jesus and more of his love!"
-Henno Smit, Pastor of Hart van Osdorp, Amsterdam, The Netherlands www.hartvanosdorp.nl

"Prophesy and Heal the Sick is Matthew's life on paper. Each chapter, story and insight is practical, authentic and extremely necessary. I have seen Matt doing this stuff while learning it myself. Not just a book to read...a book to read and do. Nike! Just do it!"
-Patrick van der Plaat, Pastor of Dianella Church of the Nazarene, Perth, Australia www.nazarene.org.au

"I used to joke that my ministry was a non-prophet ministry. However, that all changed once I spent a couple of hours with Matthew Helland. He taught me how to activate the gift of prophecy in my life. His message is simple and his methods are innovative. If you want to discover how to tap into the power of prophecy, read this book!"
-Daniel King, Evangelist, Tulsa, OK, USA www.kingministries.com

"Over the years we have brought Matt to teach at Vineyard Heroic Leadership Institute about prophetic ministry and healing prayer. He has consistently been one of our student's favorite teachers. He is a pastor at heart. I have watched him take time during activations and trainings to address the barriers of addiction, abuse and identity before moving forward with his power training. This book will inspire you to take risks and to pray, but also to both be loved and give love in a more authentic, extravagant way. Thanks for being the real deal Matt."
-Jenna Stepp, HLI/Vineyard Pilgimage Support and Co-lead of Saltwater Vineyard, Maine, USA www.godogreatthings.com and www.saltwatervineyard.org

"It has been extraordinary to see how quickly people became motivated and activated to step out and encourage others with words from God during the times Matt has taught his School of Prophecy at our church. I highly recommend this book! It comes from a man whose heart is hungry for God and lives out what he writes. It will inspire and motivate you to step out in the things of God."
-Pieter-Jan van der Wolf, Pastor of City Light Church, Alkmaar, The Netherlands www.citylightalkmaar.nl

"Matthew Helland is a gifted practitioner and a practical trainer that will inspire you to expect to see Jesus do more than you knew was possible. Prophesy and Heal the Sick will give you practical teaching, helpful practical tools, and stories that will spark you to step out and see amazing things!"
-Putty Putman, Founding Director of School of Kingdom Ministry and Teaching Pastor at The Vineyard of Central Illinois, Urbana, IL, USA www.thevineyardchurch.us

Acknowledgements

Thanks to my parents, Dean and Penny, as well as to Aaron and Michelle, my brother and sister. Thanks to you, I had a wonderful childhood. To this day, you are wonderful examples of sacrificial love and faith. I wanted to be a preacher just like my Daddy and big brother, and it is an honor to follow in their footsteps.

Thanks to the churches and leadership of the International Pentecostal Holiness Church. Thanks to Bob Cave for telling me to go to Europe and "do whatever the Holy Spirit tells you to do!" We are honored to be a part of the I.P.H.C. family.

Thanks to Bruce Foster, who mentored me in the Prophetic. Thanks for telling me, "The same Holy Spirit I have, you do to. Just do it!"

Thanks to John Wimber, who taught that "everyone gets to play", and we can all do "the stuff."

Thanks to Oral Roberts, who obeyed God's command to "Raise up your students to hear My voice, to go where My light is dim, where My voice is heard small, and My healing power is not known, even to the uttermost bounds of the earth. Their work will exceed yours, and in this I am well pleased." I am honored to be an alumnus of Oral Roberts University and endeavor to follow its mission.

Thank you to Rene and Riske de Cock and all our New Life West church family. We love making God's love tangible with you in Amsterdam Nieuw-West.

Thank you, Femke, for being the love of my life.

Thank you, Judah, Hannah, Levi, and Benjamin for being my children. I love you, and being your Papa is the greatest joy of my life.

Dedication

I want to dedicate this book my wife, Femke.
You are the greatest gift of my life.
Everything good in my life has come from you and God.
Thank you for being you.

Table of Contents

Foreword

Dr. A.D. Beacham, Jr.
Bishop of the International Pentecostal Holiness Church

For over a decade I have watched with joy, and sometimes amazement, the ministry of Matthew Helland. I really should add his family to this joy: his wife, children, brother who ministers in Brazil, and his parents.

I have had the joy of watching Matt and Femke reach out to their Muslim neighbors and friends. They have done so with respect and grace, without compromising the gospel. I heard the laughter and saw the attention of Christian as well as Muslim children, as they learned about godliness through insightful and engaging teachings from the Bible.

Over the years I have personally been blessed by words of encouragement and prophetic insight given me by Matt. Like never before, we live in a time when instant messaging and video makes it possible to communicate easily. When I see a message from Matt, I know I am hearing from a man who has spent time with God, a man who genuinely loves me and seeks the best for me, a man who has sought to determine God's timing in what, and how, he should speak.

This gift is something Matt describes in this book. It is part autobiography and part instruction. It is a lesson in discovering Holy Spirit gifts, in taking the time to develop those gifts, and humbly rejoicing and giving God glory for the effective deployment of those gifts.

I've read a lot of books about prophetic ministry, many of which are referenced by Matt. However this book is different. This book is written from the front lines of confronting the desperate needs of people in Western cultures, specifically Western Europe.

Matt is dedicating his life to raising up a new generation dedicated to the One who is "the way, the truth, and the life." They are open to the fullness of this One's Spirit. They understand this One is the Redeemer. They understand this One is Love. They know this One is Truth; and they know this One is seeking to reveal Himself to all who are thirsty in a modern spiritual desert.

What makes this book so appealing is Matt Helland's willingness to be "real." He shares his fears, lack of knowledge (and how to address it), and even his failures in exercising spiritual gifts. There is a joyful humility which runs through the book, yet it does not mask the genuine courage it takes to reach people. As you read this book, you will be inspired, informed, and I believe there will be an impartation that will take place as well.

This book shows one who is joyfully following the One. This book is real life meshed with Biblical knowledge and scholarly engagement with the culture. This is a must-read book for living out the fullness of the Spirit in our generation.

Introduction

I write this book not as a know-it-all expert but as a fellow mountain climber who delights in helping others climb higher. I have learned just like mountain climbing, growing in the prophetic and healing ministry is best done in the context of community. This is why I gladly share my successes and failures; I believe they will encourage you to grow in your ability to hear God's voice and move in His power.

I am passionate about prophecy because I am passionate about loving Jesus and loving people. Jesus healed me as a baby from Cerebral Palsy, a disease doctors said would prevent me from ever speaking or walking. Because I was healed by His Spirit, it is now my honor and privilege to speak for Him, and teach others how they can hear His voice and move in His power.

The Bible is full of Scripture exhorting us to prophesy or to speak for God. The Apostle Peter said if anyone speaks, they should speak as if they were speaking the very words of God (see 1 Peter 4:11). He also said on the day of Pentecost that in the last days God would pour out His Spirit on all flesh and everyone would prophesy (see Acts 2:17-18). Jesus said we are not to not worry whenever we are in front of leaders, for at that moment the Holy Spirit will tell us what to say (see Luke 12:11-12). He told us when we speak, our words would be his Words (10:16). The Apostle Paul explicitly states to "*follow the way of love and eagerly desire gifts of the Spirit, especially prophecy*" (1 Cor. 14:1). These are just a few of the Scriptures urging us to prophesy and flow in the gifts of the Holy Spirit.

Unfortunately, prophecy is not always present in the local Church today. Partly due to a lack of knowledge, or healthy role models to demonstrate and explain the proper use of the gifts of the Spirit. Relatively few people are willing to teach and activate other people who will move in the prophetic. Many people would like to, but just don't know how or are frightened by incorrect teaching.

In the Netherlands, people love to drink hot drinks in thin plastic cups. They do this with cup holders which enable them to drink hot coffee or tea without being burned. Consider this book as a cup holder you can use to enjoy growing in the fire of prophetic and healing ministry without getting unnecessarily burned. When training in prophecy, I aim to create a safe environment where people are challenged to step out and know they will be lovingly encouraged and corrected when necessary. This book contains guidelines to equip believers to grow in prophecy and healing ministry while keeping them and others safe.

In addition, people who grow in prophetic ministry often begin to develop other gifts of the Holy Spirit. I have personally experienced words of knowledge, words of wisdom, healing, faith, tongues, interpretation of tongues, discernment of spirits, and miracles in my life at different moments (see 1 Cor. 12:7-11).

Though every supernatural gift could have a chapter (or a book) dedicated to it, I have decided to focus on prophecy, words of knowledge, healing and power evangelism. These are the subjects I focus on most when teaching a School of Prophecy (level 1).

I have seen churches change after going through a School of Prophecy. I write this book not as an armchair theologian but as one who practices what I teach. I have been privileged to teach this material in cities across the world and have seen wonderful results. This book is full of biblical examples and modern-day stories to inspire and equip you to prophesy and heal the sick.

My attitude regarding prophetic and healing ministry is, "Everything I can do, you can do better." I have this mindset because it is the one Jesus had. We read some astounding words in John 14:12 when Jesus said, "*Very truly I tell you, whoever believes in me will do the works I have been doing, and they will do even greater things than these, because I am going to the Father*." Pause for a moment to take this in: Jesus Himself said we would do the same works He did—and even greater. He left us His Holy Spirit to empower us to do these things.

I love seeing people grow in the gifts of the Holy Spirit, in a biblical and life-giving way. I believe this book can inform, inspire, equip, activate and mobilize you to do the same things Jesus did—and greater. The gifts of the Holy Spirit are not only for "special" individuals. They are for all his children. Individuals I have trained have learned to hear the voice of God, to speak His words - and have gone on to see many healings. They, in turn, have activated other people to prophesy and heal the sick.

Near the end of a youth prophetic conference in Budapest, a young man grabbed the microphone and said, "God says I love you, I love you, I love you."

I did not brush this off as too elemental. Instead, I thought, "Yes! He caught the essence of the prophetic ministry." It revealed the passionate, loving heart of Father God who longs for His children to know Him as He truly is. He loves to speak to and through us."

Hearing God's voice is a regular part of following Jesus (see John 10:3-4). The biblical principles I share in this book will help you if you desire to grow in prophetic and healing ministry. You can grow in them if you will regularly, lovingly, and humbly use the principles I lay out. Nevertheless, the prophetic ministry is not about principles or steps, but about developing your intimate relationship with God. When we live connected to Jesus, then prophecy and the gifts of the Spirit can be normal and natural. We seek his presence first and his presents can follow.

It is my hope that you will enjoy reading this book. Even more so, it is my desire that you learn to prophesy and heal the sick! Learn to see how God can change your life and the lives of people around you when you humbly and boldly speak His words and move in the power of His Holy Spirit.

Chapter 1
Raising Up A New Generation of Prophets

"Pray for the rising up of a new generation of leaders—prophets of the apostolic mold. Leaders who could once again gather the people of God into communities of radical faithfulness." -Richard Foster, Prayer

(Prophesying over young leaders in Budapest, Hungary)

In 1978, Richard Foster was strolling across a beach in Portland, Oregon, when God literally had a conversation with him.[1] During the conversation, he noticed a large rock in the middle of the water that was being beaten by waves. It stood as a bastion of unconquerable strength.

Then he saw an ancient tree that had been hit by lightning. The tree was dead in the middle but had a few parts on the outside that were still alive. As he looked, God said to him the Church in many places looks like the ancient tree: dead in the middle with only small remnants of life on the periphery.

Then he turned again and looked at the strong rock beaten by the waves and heard God say, "But that rock is what I am calling my church to be like."

Foster writes, "I was given instructions that I assume was one of the primary reasons for the encounter. It was the guidance to pray for the rising up of a new generation of leaders—prophets of the apostolic mold. Leaders who could once again gather the people of God into communities of radical faithfulness." [2]

He goes on to describe these prophets by saying:

> What do these prophets look like? They come from every class and category of people. Some are educated; others are illiterate or semi-literate. Some come from organized churches and denominations; others come from outside these structures. Some are women, some are men, some are children.
>
> To the person they love Jesus with their whole heart. They all evidence the call of God upon their lives and the hand of God upon their ministries. It is of no consequence to them who is up front, who gets the attention, or who is remembered in the annals of history...
>
> They are insignificant and irrelevant even in the world of religion. It is not that they lack influence; it is that the place of influence is viewed as unimportant. To normal human reckoning they are little people, but in the Kingdom of God they are truly the great ones. They are the spiritual heirs of Deborah and Elijah, of Amos and Jeremiah, of Paul and the daughters of Philip.

> Under their leadership and by the power of the Holy Spirit the people of God are once again being gathered (speaking not organizationally, but organically). We are witnessing in our day a whole host of children and women and men who are getting hooked into a different order of reality and power. [3]

Foster had this encounter in 1978. I was born in 1979. When I read his words, I see my own desire to be a prophet of the apostolic mold who will gather God's people into communities of radical faithfulness. I am passionate about reaching the lost, making disciples, raising up new prophets, and life-changing communities where knowing God and hearing from Him is *normal.*

In chapter three of 1 Samuel, we read the story of God raising up a young boy named Samuel to become a prophet. Because of the poor spiritual leadership in Israel from the high priest Eli and his sons, it was uncommon for people to hear God's voice or to have spiritual visions.

"The boy Samuel ministered before the Lord under Eli. In those days the word of the Lord was rare; there were not many visions."
(1 Samuel 3:1)

God never meant it to be rare for His people to hear His voice and see visions from Him. Quite the opposite. God created us to hear His voice because He is a God who speaks. The problem is all too often we are not listening, either due to unbelief or poor spiritual leadership. For many, hearing God's voice or seeing visions from him is unreal or impossible. They lack the understanding and the tools to develop a dynamic relationship with God.

God never meant it to be rare for His people to hear His voice and see visions from Him.

When people do not know God, the Bible teaches He raises up prophets. In 1 Samuel, we read God did not just raise up one prophet, but groups of prophets. *"But when they arrived and saw Samuel leading a group of prophets who were prophesying, the Spirit of God came upon Saul's men, and they also began to prophesy."* (1 Samuel 19:20)

I have personally witnessed that it is God's intention, not to just raise up an individual prophet, but communities of prophets who regularly prophesy and can activate others to learn to hear and recognize God's voice for themselves and others.

First Samuel 10:10-11, reads, **"***When Saul and his servant arrived at Gibeah, they saw a group of prophets coming toward them. Then the Spirit of God came powerfully upon Saul, and he, too, began to prophesy. When those who knew Saul heard about it, they exclaimed, 'What? Is even Saul a prophet? How did the son of Kish become a prophet?'*"

It is not God's will for just one or two "special" people to be able to prophesy, but that *all* may prophesy. Paul writes, "*For you can* ***all*** *prophesy in turn so that everyone may be instructed and encouraged."* (1 Cor. 14:31 emphasis added)

In Acts we read, "*In the last days, God says, I will pour out my Spirit on* ***all*** *people. Your sons and daughters will prophesy, your young men will see visions, your old men will dream dreams. Even on my servants, both men and women, I will pour out my Spirit in those days, and they will prophesy*." (Acts 2:17-18 emphasis added)

Here we see the promise is for all people—males, females, young, old, poor, rich, etc.—everyone upon whom God pours out His Spirit. The new covenant God made with His people was that **everyone** could know Him. (see Jer. 31:33-34).

I was twelve-years-old when I started prophesying at a house group. My father, who was also the pastor, was full of good intentions as he shut me down because he felt I was too young to prophesy. Even though we grew up in a church that believed in the gifts of the Holy Spirit and prophecy, it was seen as mysterious and possibly dangerous. Much of this attitude had to do with a lack of knowledge and practical, positive experiences in ministering prophetically.

Yet in 1 Corinthians 14:1, Paul says we should *"follow the way of love and eagerly desire spiritual gifts, especially that we may prophesy."* Our attitude should be to eagerly desire spiritual gifts, *especially prophecy*. The Bible encourages us to prophesy in a proper and orderly way (see 1 Cor. 14:40).

In 2010, when the gifts of the Holy Spirit first started functioning regularly in my life, I found myself doubting. Was it God's will for me to prophesy? Was what I felt some trick of the devil, or maybe my own prideful desire? Then I read Paul's word saying to *eagerly* desire spiritual gifts and I wrote in my journal: "GOD, I WANT TO PROPHESY! I WANT TO HEAL THE SICK!"

The next morning, I was on Facebook chatting with someone when I felt led to ask him, "Do you have pain in your right foot?

He asked, "How did you know that?"

I picked up the phone and called him. All the pain in his foot disappeared the moment I prayed for him.

God wants us to desire the gifts of the Spirit, especially prophecy. However, there are some formidable hindrances which can keep us from growing in prophetic ministry.

Hindrances to Develop Prophetic Ministry: #1 An Unbiblical World View

One reason many believers do not experience a dynamic relationship with God is because their world view is based more on ideas from the 18th century Enlightenment, than from Scripture. Four big ideas from that time are atheism (or deism), rationalism, materialism, and individualism.[4]

Atheism or deism is the idea God does not exist, and even if He does, He is not involved in our daily lives. Instead, He is more of a Creator who, like a clock maker, set things in motion but is otherwise uninvolved in His creation.

Rationalism says if you cannot rationally explain something, you should not trust it. Rationalism rules out all biblical and modern miracles (the virgin birth, the resurrected Savior, divine healing, etc.). People who subscribe to a purely rationalistic viewpoint presuppose we live in a closed world-system in which the supernatural does not and cannot exist.

Materialism says ‘only what you can experience with your five senses exists.’ Many funerals I have attended in the Netherlands never mention anything about life-after-death since materialism implies once a person dies, it’s all over.

Individualism is the idea that it is most important for you to believe in yourself first above any other person or ideas. This individualism, taken to the extreme, engenders not only pride but greed, selfishness, and all the kinds of brokenness our world experiences today.

Western cultures are far greater adherents to the Enlightenment than to the teachings of the Bible, including many Christians who have unknowingly bought into these ideas. Their core beliefs are not from the Bible, but their culture.

The Bible reveals a personal God who desires to interact with us daily and is intimately familiar with every detail of our lives, including the very number of hairs on our heads (see Luke 12:7). It teaches using our five senses are important, yet there is more than our five physical senses can experience or understand (see Ephesians 3:20). It teaches there is a spiritual dimension to our being, and it is through our spirits we personally know God; and learn to use our spiritual senses as well as our physical ones. It also explains that though it may be important to have a healthy self-image, the purpose of our existence is to live in community with God and with others. No man is an island, and everyone longs for a perfect and unconditional love which can only be found through knowing Jesus Christ. Knowing Jesus awakens the supernatural element in our lives which makes living for God both natural and supernatural.

Barrier #2 Misunderstanding Between Prophecy in the Old Testament and in the New Testament

Another source of misunderstanding is when people confuse Old Testament prophecy with New Testament prophecy. In the Old Testament, prophets generally declared judgment, and if they made a mistake they could be stoned (see Deut. 18:20-22). In the New Testament, prophecy is primarily believers strengthening, encouraging, and comforting one another. There is no death penalty hanging on the necks of those who don't prophesy accurately. However, every prophetic word *must* be evaluated and tested to determine what is from God and what is not (see 1 Cor. 14:29; 1 Thess. 5:19-22).

Not understanding the difference between Old Testament and New Testament prophecy is a common barrier preventing people from growing in prophetic ministry. Who is going to prophesy if you are afraid of making a mistake and being stoned as a false prophet? How can a person develop in this ministry if they have no sound paradigm for New Testament prophecy? This book is an attempt at laying down a sound and biblical structure for developing prophetic ministry.

When people prophesy, preach, or do evangelism using an Old Testament paradigm, they can be highly destructive. Understanding grace and the Gospel of Jesus Christ is extremely important for those who speak God's words. The Gospel is not about changing your outward behavior or appearance, but your heart being transformed by the love and grace of God. Prophecy should never destroy people or a church. It should serve to build the Church up (see 1 Cor. 14:4).

There are times when God can use someone to bring words of warning and correction to an individual or a church. However, these words must be married with hope and life. In Revelation chapters two through three, Jesus brings words of correction to seven churches in Asia Minor. These words are woven together with words of encouragement and promises of the rewards God has for them if they obey Him. The prophetic ministry should never bring condemnation or death to individuals, but should bring hope and life even if there are words of correction involved.

As parents of our children, we regularly bring correction to them in the context of a deep, loving relationship. Nobody else can correct my children as my wife and I can because no one else loves them like we do. Correcting other people's children is not always good or effective because of a lack of relationship. Discipline without a relationship can lead to rebellion. This is why focusing on the most basic form of prophetic ministry (strengthening, encouraging, and comforting) is best for everyone desiring to grow in this vital ministry.

Barrier #3 Misunderstanding What Prophecy Encompasses

Prophecy is not just foretelling the future, but also forthtelling what God thinks about a person or situation. Prophecy that is predictive is foretelling. Prophecy which declares the thoughts and intentions of God's heart and the revelation of His will for a situation, a person, a place, or a situation is known as forthtelling.[5] It can be very similar to preaching. In fact, the first Protestant manual on preaching written in 1592 by William Perkins was called, *"The Art of Prophesying."*[6]

Prophecy is not just foretelling the future, but also forthtelling what God thinks about a person or situation.

Prophesying is communicating God's heart through words and deeds. God can speak about the present, past or future. There are different levels of prophetic ministry, and though not every believer is a prophet, every believer can learn to hear the voice of God and speak His words. Every believer can and should encourage, strengthen, and comfort one another with words from God (see 1 Cor. 14:3). Prophecy has everything to do with knowing and connecting to God's heart. Every true prophetic word will then line up with His written Word in Scripture.

Being able to experience God's voice and power is truly life changing. Everything changes when prayer is no longer a religious obligation, but a two-way conversation with God. He is always speaking - in many ways. It is wonderful to learn how to connect with Him daily.

(Prophecy has to do with connecting to the Father Heart of God.)

Prophecy in Scripture is knowing and seeing God. Proverbs 29:18 says God's people perish because of a lack of revelation or prophetic vision. One Dutch version translates Proverbs 29:18 as, *"God's people perish because of a lack of prophecy"* (Nederlands, NBV). Obviously, God's people are not perishing because they are not foretelling the future—they are perishing because they know *about* God, but they don't know Him. As Hosea 4:6 says, *"My people perish because they don't know me"* (NLT).

Prophecy in the broadest sense is simply hearing, seeing, sensing, and knowing God and then at times telling others what we have heard and seen from Jesus (see Rev. 19:10). Prophecy is a normal part of developing a healthy prayer life. We talk to God, and He talks to us. Hearing the voice of God and speaking his words (prophecy) should be normal for every believer.

Prophecy in the broadest sense is simply hearing, seeing, sensing, and knowing God and then at times telling others what we have heard and seen from Jesus.

Barrier #4: Fear of the Gifts of the Holy Spirit and False Teaching

"Which of you fathers, if your son asks for a fish, will give him a snake instead? Or if he asks for an egg, will give him a scorpion? If you then, though you are evil, know how to give good gifts to your children, how much more will your Father in heaven give the Holy Spirit to those who ask him!" Luke 11:11-13

I recall teaching some teenagers about the Holy Spirit. When I used the word Holy Spirit they started talking about ghosts and things they were afraid of. I knew treating the Holy Spirit this way would make them incapable of flowing in His gifts, so I showed them that the Holy Spirit only gives *good* gifts. We must never fear anything which truly comes from the Holy Spirit. Among His assignments on earth, the Holy Spirit came to comfort us, to teach us, and to empower us (see John 14:16, 26 and Acts 1:8).

A young person told me, none of Paul's letters mention anything supernatural. He said this proved miracles, signs, and wonders are no longer for today. I showed him entire chapters in Paul's epistles which instruct us to grow in the gifts of the Holy Spirit and use signs and wonders to share our faith.

He had been taught God does not do anything supernatural because we have the Bible. This false teaching is based on people's experience of never seeing God do something supernatural. It is incorrect to create a teaching on our experience and not upon what the Bible teaches.

People may fear the gifts of the Holy Spirit due to stories of abuses and false teachings propagated by false teachers or false prophets. They throw away the baby with the dirty bath water. Please, throw out dirty water, but do not get rid of the Spirit's gifts because some people have abused and misused them.

Driving a car can also be dangerous. Yet we still drive cars in a safe way. The gifts of the Holy Spirit used in an incorrect manner can be disruptive and dangerous. So, we need to learn how to use them in a safe manner. As Paul said, *"Be eager to prophesy, and do not forbid speaking in tongues. But everything should be done in a fitting and orderly way"* (1 Cor. 14:39-40). Each of us can walk in the gifts of the Spirit in a way that is life-giving and orderly. We can use them lovingly, humbly and often.

Barrier #5 Thinking I Must Feel, Hear, or See Something Before Prophesying

We do not have to work up our emotions, feel the anointing, speak in King James English, or fall into a trance to prophesy. All gifts from God—including salvation, healing, tongues, words of knowledge, and prophecy—work by faith (see Eph. 2:8-9)

We may be speaking the very words of God, but we don't have to be weird doing it. We are to speak trusting that God will inspire our words (see 1 Peter 4:11). Speaking God's words should be *normal.* Simply begin by praying for people in a way that strengthens, encourages, and comforts them. *Everyone* can prophesy at this basic level.

One leader of a large Pentecostal church told me that he could only prophesy at the end of meetings. This is when he could *feel* the anointing and his faith was high. Yet the Bible says that we operate by faith, and not by what we see or feel (see 2 Cor. 5:7). We can open our mouths and trust God to fill them (see Psalm 81:10). When we open our mouths, prophecy may start as a small trickle from a faucet, but as we continue it may begin to flow like a river.

Smith Wigglesworth was once at a church meeting where, after sitting in prayer quietly, he began speaking God's words fluently and easily as if liquid fire was flowing from his lips. The leaders at the end of the service remarked, "How quickly you are moved by the Spirit! What is your secret? Do please tell us." They were somewhat astounded at his blunt reply: "Well, you see, it is like this. If the Spirit does not move me, I move the Spirit."[7]

As John Booth, founder of the Salvation Army said, "I am not waiting for a move of God, I am a move of God."[8]

Paul said that the "*spirit of prophets are under the control of prophets*" (see 1 Cor. 14:32). This means that we are the ones who initiate prophecy. If we wait for God to come and force our tongue to move, we will never speak.

If we say that we believe in prophecy or healing and never prophesy or heal the sick; we probably don't believe we can. Belief without actions is dead (see James 5:17). What a person does shows what they truly believe and not only what they say they believe.

To move in the Spirit, we do not need an angel to sit on our head or any supernatural manifestations to take place. Wigglesworth once said, "I am not moved by what I feel. I am not moved by what I see. I am moved only by what I believe. I cannot understand God by feelings. I understand God by what the Word says about Him." [9]

Through faith in God and his word, we can prophesy and heal the sick. The Bible instructs us to heal the sick and to be eager to prophesy (see Matt. 10:8 & 1 Cor. 14:39). We do not have to wait for a feeling or sign. We simply step out and begin speaking while trusting our Heavenly Father to, together with us, take the wheel. It is easier to steer a moving car than a stopped one.

Open your mouth and trust God to fill it. Trust that if you ask God for bread, He will not give you a stone. Trust that he can speak through you.

Everybody Gets to Play

Any parent would be disappointed to find all the Christmas and birthday presents they bought for a child stored up in a closet having never been touched by their child. God has many "spiritual" gifts for his children to use but that are not being opened and played with. The gifts of the Holy Spirit are for all of his children, and as John Wimber used to say, "everybody gets to play." Everybody can prophesy, heal the sick, get a word of knowledge, cast out demons, etc. (see Mark 16:15-18).

The gifts of the Holy Spirit are *gifts*. They do not depend on us earning points or being "good." They are given to us by grace, which we receive and use by faith (see Eph. 2:8-9). We prophesy because God loves to speak to people through us.

Romans 12:6 in the Living Bible explains it so: *"If God has given you the ability to prophesy, then prophesy whenever you can -- as often as your faith is strong enough to receive a message from God."*

As I developed this gift (together with God) in me, I learned to love to prophesy whenever I can and as often as possible. I love to receive a word or picture from the Lord for my life and for the lives of others. We do not have to work up emotions or feel something special to prophesy. We can open our mouths by faith and deliver a life-giving word from God to someone.

If one hundred people stood before me, I could trust God that he could enable me to prophesy over all of them. However, I would rather train five other people so that we could all serve twenty individuals instead of one person prophesying over one hundred. Like Samuel and Elijah, I am passionate about training up schools or groups of believers who can prophesy.

You can also hear God's voice and speak His words. You can prophesy! What is hindering you?

(Dutch prophetic ministry team that helped serve churches in Budapest.)

Schools of Prophecy

In 2010, I led my first School of Prophecy in southern Oklahoma together with an experienced prophet. I was amazed to see how large groups of people of all ages began boldly, accurately, and scripturally prophesying. Since that first School of Prophecy, I have led similar schools in places such as Amsterdam, Budapest, Barcelona, Oklahoma, New England, Czech Republic, Kiev, and California. I have seen hundreds of people activated and growing in accurate and life-giving prophetic ministry.

The gift of prophecy, like every other skill, is something we grow in by practicing. If you want to shoot a basketball accurately, you must spend hundreds of hours practicing your jump shot. If you want to prophesy regularly and accurately, you should regularly pray, study the Bible, fast, and prophesy. Your identity must be anchored in the Gospel, and your mind should be full of Scripture, so what is inside of you will come out. You must also be open to feedback.

As I have mentioned before, I believe God wants to raise up groups of prophets. I now have an ever-growing group on my phone called Profeten ("prophets" in Dutch). This is a group of over twenty individuals in the Netherlands who all have a strong prophetic gifting. If I need a traveling ministry team, I can ask them for help.

Prophets are not called to be hidden alone in caves but to work and serve each other in groups or teams. They are not to compete with one another; instead, they complete each other. Like the prophets Judas and Silas, they encourage and strengthen churches (see Acts 15:32). They are to equip believers to be able to prophesy and hear God's voice for themselves.

In February 1959, Jesus Christ visited Kenneth Hagin for an hour and a half. Jesus told him, "I did not put prophets in the Church to guide the New Testament Church. My Word says, 'As many as are led by the Spirit of God, they are the sons of God' [Rom. 8:14]. Now if you listen to Me, I am going to teach you how to follow My Spirit. Then I want you to teach my people how to be led by the Spirit."[10]

It is unhealthy if a believer is too dependent on a prophet, counselor, pastor, or leader providing direction from God. We can each learn to be led primarily by the Spirit of God inside of us and through Scripture. We do not look to prophets first for direction in our lives. We look to God first and secondarily to other people who know Him and will confirm what He speaks to our own hearts. As Hagin once said, "Do not build your life on prophecies. Do not guide your life by prophecies. Build your life on the Word! Let those other things be secondary. Put the Word of God first!"[11]

The Goal of Prophetic Ministry: Knowing Jesus and Making Him Known

People frequently ask me, "Does God have a future partner for me?"

I learned to answer this question by stating something like, "I see someone with whom you can have a life-changing, amazing, mutually-loving future with. This person loves you so much that He willingly sacrificed all He had to be with you. His name is Jesus Christ."

The goal of prophetic ministry is never just finding out information or knowledge; instead, it is about knowing Jesus (see Rev. 19:10).

The goal of prophetic ministry is never just finding out information or knowledge; instead, it is about knowing Jesus.

Matthew 7:20-23 describes the day of judgment where many people will state that they prophesied, healed the sick, and cast out demons. If we do all these things and yet do not know Him, Jesus will answer, *"Away from me, I never knew you."*

There is a danger that prayer or prophecy can become all about us using God to *get* things from Him.

Once I sat for an hour in silent prayer and caught myself asking Him for information or a secret that would be useful for me. I wanted something from Him to reward my valuable time investment. Instead, I felt Him gently rebuke me by saying, "My son, I want you to just be with me and enjoy me. Don't be so caught up with doing things, but simply enjoy being with me as I enjoy you."

The greatest thing I can get through prayer is God himself. If I have God, then I have everything I need (see Psalm 23:1 and Matt. 6:33).

In a world so full of brokenness, division, and empty answers, humanity longs for real solutions to our problems. We desire wholeness, unconditional love, unity, joy and true fulfillment. Yet we waste our time and energy going after things that we do not really need and that do not truly satisfy.

Knowing Jesus is the key to true satisfaction in life. Prophecy is not about prophecy, but about *knowing Jesus*.

Jesus Christ offers everything our heart desires. However, the world needs to see individuals who flesh this out in their daily lives. They need to see examples of people who truly know and live with God.

The goal of prophecy is knowing Jesus and making Him known. God calls us into a living relationship with Jesus (see 1 Cor. 1:9). We grow in prophecy by following the Apostle John's example of laying our head on the chest of Jesus (see John 13:23).

> The goal of prophecy is knowing Jesus and making Him known.

God, the greatest lover, desires to share His secrets with us, and humbly drawing near to Him through prayer, Scripture, meditation, silence, and other spiritual disciplines is a way that we can regularly place our heads on the chest of Jesus. It is through intimacy with Jesus that we are empowered to speak His words to others.

A young girl at a church once asked me, "How do you do that prophesying?"

I answered, "If your mother called you on the phone, would you recognize her voice?"

"Yes, I would," she responded.

"Well, that is the same with me and Jesus. I spend a lot of time listening to His voice, and I often recognize when He wants to tell me something for myself or for others."

The goal of prophecy is *knowing God.* This is the heart of prophecy, and prophets are to live so close to God that His words become their words.

God intends for a new generation of prophets to rise up. Not every believer is a prophet, but every believer should be able to experience God's voice and direction in their daily lives. Hearing God's voice is not just for inside church walls, but for improving every sphere of society.

Hearing God's Voice Changes Your World

When Amos Landers asked God what he should do after he had lost his job, he heard God say, "Wash windows!"

Landers, in obedience to God's voice, started a window washing business that cleans window in businesses and major high rises of cities in Oklahoma and Kansas.[12]

Another friend of mine, Dermatologist Dr. Steven Smith, had an amazing way of developing a medicine for skin sicknesses. His wife heard the name of two chemicals, bromide and nickel during prayer. She did not know what they were, but Dr. Smith did. Through much scientific research and testing he proceeded to develop a new medicine called Lomalux. This medicine has helped thousands of people around the world deal with psoriasis, eczema, and acne.[13]

Frank Laubach and George Washington Carver are two other examples of men who have made a huge contribution to society by listening and obeying God's voice. Laubach did an experiment with a notebook and pen to see if he could write down every time he felt God speaking to him. He determined to see if he could always live in constant contact with God. His little experiment led him not only to connect deeper with God, but also to develop an entire literacy program which has helped millions of people around the world learn to read.[14]

George Washington Carver was an African-American man living during the 19th century in the deep south of the United States. He revolutionized the agricultural industry with his scientific research and inventions. His secret was his relationship with God. He once said, "I love to think of nature as an unlimited broadcasting station, through which God speaks to us every hour if we will only tune in."

He once had the following conversation with God: "Mr. Creator, show me the secrets of your universe."

"Little man," God replied, "you're not big enough to know the secrets of My universe, but I'll show you the secret of the peanut."

Carver went on to invent over three hundred products from the peanut. His greatest passion was not making money, but serving God and humankind.

He called his laboratory God's Little Workshop and he, together with God, made discoveries there that literally changed the agricultural world of his time.[15] He was an inventor, an educator, a botanist, and, most importantly, a friend of God.

William Wilberforce was another man mightily used by God. He was very influential in stopping slavery in the British Empire. One day he had a significant conversation with John Newton, a former slave trader and author of the hymn "Amazing Grace." Newton told him, "God has raised you up for the good of the church and the good of the nation... continue in Parliament, who knows that but for such a time as this God has brought you into public life and has a purpose for you."[16]

Wilberforce's political career was highly influenced by the Quakers and by John Wesley, the founder of the Methodist or Holiness movement. Wilberforce was a prophetic voice in England's parliament who gave his life to abolish slavery and change his society. The United States suffered a civil war to end slavery, but a man influenced by powerful Christian movements of his time spearheaded England's abolitionist movement.

It took nearly three decades for Wilberforce to achieve his goal of abolishing slavery. In fact, only three days before he died in 1807, the British Empire abolished slavery thanks in large part to the Spirit-inspired efforts of Wilberforce.

We need prophets who will reveal God's heart and design for every area of society—people who will speak up against issues such as injustice, human trafficking, and poverty. We need people who will be a voice for those who have no voice and will dare to go where no one else wants to go.

I love the story of Gladys May Aylward. As a young girl, Aylward felt God calling her to spend her life in China telling people about Jesus.[17] After applying to go with a Christian mission, she was denied because her academic background was too weak. They said she would never be able to learn the language and could not pass the Bible courses. She was also too old to be a missionary.

Aylward believed she heard God, though, and she sold all she had to buy a one-way ticket to China. There, she helped the local government put a stop to foot binding, a horrible practice that crippled women for life. She helped stop prison riots and was a noted advocate for the poor.

She adopted many orphan children personally. Once she started taking in orphans, she found herself with a large group of children—an orphanage! In 1938, when the Japanese invaded China, she led over one hundred orphans to safety, after being wounded herself. She was honored by the local government and able to make a significant impact on the lives of many in that region of China. Aylward could do this because she listened to and obeyed the voice of God.

Every week, my wife and I spend significant time with prostitutes in the Red-Light District of Amsterdam. Many of these individuals were abused and ended up in this line of work due to difficult circumstances in their lives. Their work, though legalized in the Netherlands, is full of hardships and injustices. Our goal is to share God's love with them and help them find true freedom and a new life in Christ.

We have seen people set free from this lifestyle and step into the freedom of knowing Christ because of believers who reach out to them with love and friendship. This is what Jesus did and what we should do (see Matthew 21:31).

Prophecy is about knowing the heart of God and speaking His words over individuals, families, churches, businesses, and nations. It is knowing the heart of God, obeying His promptings and teaching others to do the same.

The greatest resource we have available is not money, strategies, or human machinations but knowing God Himself and experiencing His power. When we know God and can communicate His words (prophecy), all things are possible.

Chapter 2

Three Prerequisites For Prophetic Ministry: Love, Courage, and Humility

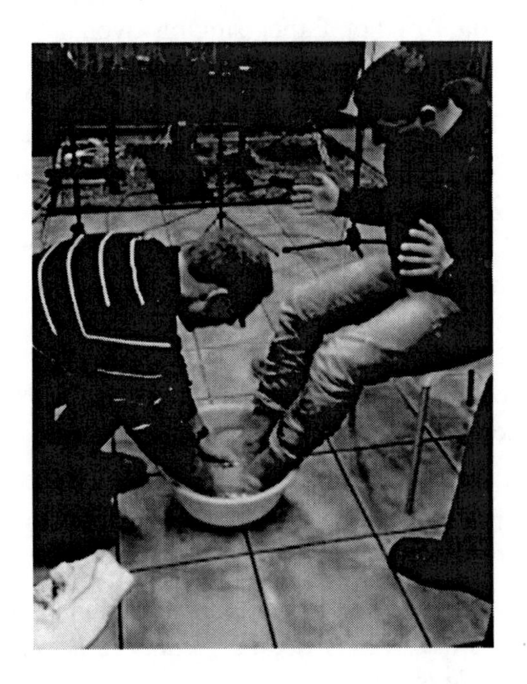

(Washing the feet of a leader in Barcelona, Spain.)

"The only thing that counts is faith expressing itself through love."
Gal. 5:6b

"The LORD your God is in your midst, a mighty one who will save; he will rejoice over you with gladness; he will quiet you by his love; he will exult over you with loud singing." ***Zephaniah 3:17, ESV***

When my daughter, Hannah, was born, her mother had lost too much blood to be able to hold her in her arms. My sweet little girl came out crying at the top of her lungs, as all new-born babies should. When the nurses handed her to me, I started singing a song that my father sang over me. I sang: *"I love Hannah. I love Hannah, yes I do. Yes I do. She is very special. She is very special. Yes she is. Yes she is."*

The moment she heard my voice, she stopped crying because she recognized the voice of her father singing over her. I had sung and spoken over her when she was inside of her mother's belly.

When our youngest, Benjamin, was a baby, there were moments that he would stop crying when his big sister Hannah started singing over him: *"I love Benjamin. I love Benjamin. Yes, I do. Yes, I do. He is very special. He is very special. Yes, he is."* Benjamin would often stop crying immediately.

This is a wonderful picture of what prophecy is all about. Prophecy is about loving people the way that God loves us. It is singing the song of love over others that God continually sings over us.

Prophecy is about loving people the way that God loves us.

Another day I as I walked into the house, Hannah began singing, "*I love Papa. I love Papa. Yes, I do. Yes, I do. He is very special. He is very special. Yes, He is."*

My heart leaped for joy as she sang to me the song I sang to her! This is a wonderful picture of how worship touches the heart of our Father God. The heart of prophecy is all about being loved and loving others the way that God loves us.

In Numbers 11:20-30 we read a story of seventy elders of Israel who began prophesying when the Holy Spirit came upon them. All of them prophesied at the assigned tent where they were to meet Moses - except for Eldad and Medad, who remained in their homes. To Joshua's horror, these two elders were prophesying freely at the wrong location, and he demanded that Moses silence them immediately.

Moses unexpectedly responded to Joshua by saying, *"Are you jealous for my sake? I wish that all the Lord's people were prophets and that the Lord would put his Spirit upon them all!" (Numbers 11:29)*

This amazing narrative not only is a preview of the Day of Pentecost when God would pour out His Spirit upon all flesh, it also has an important key hidden in the names of Eldad and Medad. Eldad's name means "God has loved" and Medad's name means "love."[18] Whenever and wherever we prophesy, we must prophesy in love. Prophecy without love is meaningless.

Prophecy without love is meaningless.

Paul makes this clear in 1 Corinthians 13 when he says:

> *If I could speak all the languages of earth and of angels, but didn't love others, I would only be a noisy gong or a clanging cymbal. If I had the gift of prophecy, and if I understood all of God's secret plans and possessed all knowledge, and if I had such faith that I could move mountains, but didn't love others, I would be nothing. If I gave everything I have to the poor and even sacrificed my body, I could boast about it; but if I didn't love others, I would have gained nothing. 1 Cor. 13:1-3*

In January 2016, I took a Dutch ministry team to do a large prophetic youth conference in Budapest, Hungary. I took one of my best friends who grew up in a traditional background where he had heard very little about prophesying. When I told him that he was going to prophesy, he told me that he was going to watch me and learn but that by no means was he ready to prophesy.

At the end of that first meeting, a line of fifty people lined up to receive prophetic ministry. I stood there with an interpreter and my friend, who was on the other side watching and listening as I prophesied over the first individual. Then I simply walked away and left him there with a line waiting to receive a word from God through him!

He started prophesying over all of those people and afterward told me, "Matt, this was so easy. All I had to do was love these people the way that God loves me. It was so easy and so amazing!" I knew that he was already full of the love, Scripture, and the Spirit of God. For him, prophesying would be very natural and easy.

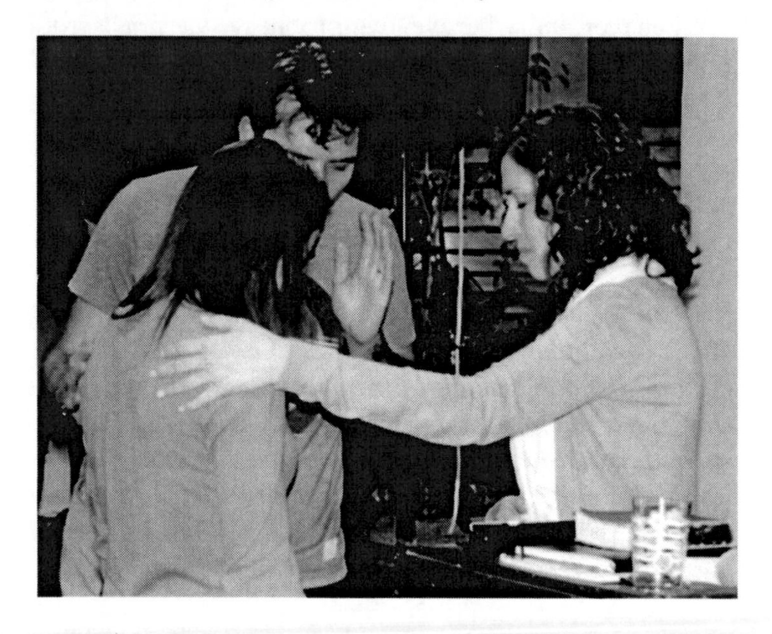

(When you are full of God's Word and His Spirit then prophesying can be very easy.)

Once, I trained a team in Fresno, California, to share the good news of Jesus using the gifts of the Holy Spirit, which I call Power Evangelism, at a local mall. Evangelism is a word feared and hated by Christians and non-Christians alike because their idea of evangelism is being a pushy, know-it-all Christian who stands up on a soapbox and tells everyone to repent or they will burn in hell. That is **NOT** evangelism.

Evangelism is telling people the good news that will make their lives better. The goal of evangelism is to draw people closer to Jesus by making His message of love, power, and restoration tangible. It does entail speaking about sin and brokenness that we all face, but it is done in the context of hope, faith, and love.

My favorite power evangelist that evening was a twelve-year-old boy. Everyone accepted his offer to pray for them! People's bodies were healed when he prayed for them, and a whole lot of people that evening had tears well up in their eyes when he, along with other team members, simply expressed God's love to them.

Evangelism and prophecy are not difficult because they are both about simply loving people, the way God loves us. If we are connected to God, prophecy and evangelism becomes natural and normal. When the Gospel is at the core of our identity, they are not things we *do* but something we *are*.

This will not be the case, however, when people have a distorted view of the Gospel. I have seen people do evangelism with an Old Testament "turn or burn" approach, which is not only unscriptural, but extremely damaging. God does call us to repentance, but it is through His kindness (see Rom. 2:4). Jesus said that God is *"kind to the ungrateful and wicked"* (Luke 6:35a). We are to be merciful just as our heavenly Father is merciful (see Luke 6:35b, 36). We are to be kind to people who doubt (see Jude 1:22). Mercy triumphs over judgment, and we are to overcome evil with good (see James 2:13, Rom. 12:21). God sent Jesus into the world not to condemn the world, but to save it (see John 3:17). We should follow His example.

Those who prophesy and evangelize must function first and foremost from a paradigm of encouraging, strengthening and comforting their hearers and not judgment, as did many Old Testament Prophets (see 1 Cor. 14:3). The goal of prophecy and evangelism is bringing people good news, which can change their lives. We are to be like salt that makes people thirsty to taste the living water that Jesus has to offer.

The goal of prophecy and evangelism is bringing people good news, which can change their lives.

In college, I once went to stand outside of heavy metal Marilyn Manson concert to talk and pray to concertgoers. Marilyn Manson was known for ripping up a Bible at his concerts and performing other shock antics for his audiences. With my youth group, we hoped we could pray and reach out to the concertgoers. Unfortunately, we were not the only Christians who decided to show up. At the entrance was a group of Christians with a large bull horn and a painting of hell telling all the visitors that they were on their way there. Understandably, no one wanted to talk to us because they thought we were a part of their group.

However, there was another group of Christians that could pray with concertgoers. These were Oral Roberts University students who wisely dressed in black and could connect to concertgoers. At the end of the evening, there was a conflict between the last group of Christians and the first. One of the ladies declared that the other group of Christians was going to hell because they were dressed in black. Obviously, this well-intentioned woman had no idea that the Gospel is not at all about what color clothes a person wears but has everything to do with the sacrificial act of love Jesus suffered on the cross.

Evangelism and prophetic ministry should always be pursued along with an understanding of what the good news of Jesus Christ is all about. Our identity should be firmly rooted and grounded in the love of Christ and not in outward signs of behavior or results.

In his School of Kingdom Ministry Manual, Putty Putman describes the process for a believer to grow in power evangelism.[19] The first and most critical step is that people's identities must be securely grounded in the Gospel of Jesus Christ. If this does not take place, a person's life and ministry may be on a destructive path.

An example of this is when someone tells a person they are not healed because it is their own fault for lacking faith. Another danger is that if a prophetic word does not take place as they think it should, a person may become discouraged or even devastated. This is why healthy guidelines are necessary when prophesying and receiving prophetic ministry. Our faith should be solidly founded upon what Jesus did for us on the cross and not on whether we get healed or a prophetic word comes to pass the way we want it to or in the timing we desire.

Praying for the sick and prophecy aims to loving and encourage people no matter what may or may not happen. We should not pull people down or shame them, but should always build them up. Even when I may have a word of correction or warning for someone, my goal is to convey this in a manner that strengthens, encourages, honors, and builds them up.

Henri Nouwen is a beloved Dutch priest whose life message was all about knowing that we are the beloved of God.[20] His message was that the world tries to label us with three lies: "You are what you do. You are what you have. You are what people think of you."

All three of these statements can be harrowing and destructive in that they can lead to insecurity, fear, and pride. Nouwen said that the core of Christian faith is that we can hear the voice of Father God speaking over us as He did over Jesus at His baptism, saying, *"You are my dearly beloved Child. I love you and I am pleased with you" (Matthew 3:17).*

Growing up, I watched my father and mother pastor, teach, and serve many people. They taught me through their words and example that the most important thing you can do is love people. Our most important skill is not how well we preach, teach, or heal the sick; it's how we love people. We love others as God loves us. Expressing the love of God in our words and deeds is of the utmost importance to how we lead our lives.

> Our most important skill is not how well we preach, teach, or heal the sick; it's how we love people.

Inevitably, everyone I train in prophecy will mention at some point in their prophecies that God says, "I love you." I have seen the people on the streets of major European cities (such as Barcelona, Amsterdam, Budapest, etc.) have tears well up in their eyes when they hear this truth. Prophecy is all about expressing the loving heart of Father God to people in a way that they can receive and understand it.

> Prophecy is all about expressing the loving heart of Father God to people in a way that they can receive and understand it.

God's Love: Radical and Sacrificial

Loving people as God loves us requires radical and sacrificial love. It may cost us to love people, but it is always worth it.

The great Indian Christian, Sadhu Sundar Singh, was once travelling on a snowy cold mountainside late at night together with a companion. They needed to get to the next village before they literally froze to death. However, they found another traveler who was already freezing and nearly dead.

Singh said, "Come on, let us pick him and save him."

The other responded, "Forget it. If we carry him then we will all die. You can try to save him, but I am going to save myself!"

Singh had a difficult choice to face. Was he going to carry the dying man or let him die? He chose to pick him up on his shoulder and try to save him at the risk of losing his own life.

He chose to walk with the man draped over his shoulder. He thought he was going to die. However, due to his body heat the other man warmed up and was soon walking along side of him. What they found to their astonishment, though, was the friend who had abandoned them to save himself was lying face down frozen in the snow. Singh's body heat had kept them both alive, but the man who tried to save himself froze to death. [21]

This is what Jesus meant when He said those who save their lives will lose it, but those who lose their lives for Him will save it (Matt. 16:25). We must learn to love as Christ loves us. We must pray that we are able to love people even when they may despise us or hate us.

Courage: Faith to Take Risks

I was being interviewed on a television show when I started getting a pain in the back of my head by my neck. I realized this was probably a word of knowledge I needed to release for someone to receive healing. I had never done something like this before. As I watched the clock tick away, I stepped out and said, "I believe that there is someone who has something on their back on their neck right here and that God is healing you right now."[22]

When the program was over, I thought to myself, "What in the world did I just do?!"

Three weeks later, I was told that the man behind the camera was healed when I gave that word! More importantly, words of knowledge and all kinds of healings started taking place at nearly every meeting I spoke at during that time. This would not have been activated in my life in that way if I had not opened my mouth and taken a risk. God honors faith, and faith is being able to take risks.

God honors faith, and faith is being able to take risks.

Gary Best in *Naturally Supernatural* gives a great illustration of this principle.[23] He tells about a vision he had during prayer where he found himself on a high diving board above a large swimming pool with no water inside of it. In this vision, he hears God say, "Jump!"

"God there is no water in the swimming pool. That is really going to hurt," he responds.

God says, "Jump!"

"But God?!" Best responds.

God says, *"Jump!"*

Best jumps. At the moment he jumps, the swimming pool is filled with water. As the late John Wimber always said, "Faith is spelled R-I-S-K."

As stated in chapter one, prophecy is activated and operated by faith and not by feelings or emotions. I have seen people work up their emotions to "feel God," yet I do not have to *feel* anything to prophesy, get a word of knowledge, speak in tongues, or pray for the sick. Prophets function by faith and not primarily by feelings.

Prophets function by faith and not primarily by feelings.

This may mean we do things even when we are afraid. Courage does not mean we don't experience fear. It means we do things *despite our fears*. Every time I go to talk to strangers on the streets, I fear what they may think or say of me. It is scary. It is also highly rewarding getting to see people healed, or get to know Christ because I had the courage to talk to them. One of my common prayers is, "God, let my faith in you always be greater than my fear."

"God, let my faith in you always be greater than my fear."

Humility: The Power of God Under the Control of Love

My other prayer is "God help me to always remain humble." Moses was one of the greatest prophets of the Bible and he is described as, *"a very humble man, more humble than anyone else on the face of the earth."* (Numbers 12:3).

Jesus said, *"learn from me, for I am gentle and humble in heart, and you will find rest for your souls"* (see Matt. 11:29). We reflect Jesus, and He is "*gentle and humble in heart."* Moses and Jesus are the best models of effective prophetic ministry and they were both humble.

When we look at Jesus, we see our Heavenly Father (see John 14:9). Jesus is God the Father's selfie! As followers of Jesus, we must be able to say to others, *"Imitate me, as I imitate Christ"* (1 Cor. 11:1). Jesus Christ was humble and when I am prideful, rude or arrogant, I am not reflecting Him.

Being prophetic is never an excuse for being rude, unkind, arrogant, or not accountable to authority. This is why I always try to smile and be friendly when I am prophesying. I am also always accountable to the leaders of a church when I serve them by preaching, teaching, and prophesying.

To prophesy, we must have a high level of courage, love, and humility. Leaving one of these three out of our ministry will ensure either a short-lived, destructive, or ineffective ministry.

(I always try to smile when prophesying over people.)

In 2010 when the gifts of the Holy Spirit began to develop in my life, God spoke to me through a woman who had learned to hear from Him, "I have taught you what it is to move in my power, but now I will teach you what it is to move in my power under control."

Since then I have learned that *humility* is the definition for moving in the power of the Holy Spirit under the control of love.

> I have learned that *humility* is the definition for moving in the power of the Holy Spirit under the control of love.

I was at a church in Oklahoma where years earlier I had experienced a powerful move of God. As I prepared for the meeting, I found myself becoming nervous and insecure. I started asking God, "Could you give me an awesome word of knowledge? Could you give me the key to unlocking something so that your power and presence will be experienced this morning really powerfully?"

Suddenly I realized I was operating from a sense of insecurity and pride. It was all about me and not about Jesus. I had to repent and simply relax and focus on ministering from a place of security, love, and humility.

Jonathan Edwards once gave a wonderful description of what pride and humility look like. He placed the two as polar opposites against each other. The chart here illustrates what pride and humility is.[24]

Pride is...	Humility is...
...being driven by emptiness or fear.	...being content.
...being disrespectful to people who think or act differently than yourself.	...being kind, friendly and respectful even to people who are different than yourself.
...being unteachable. Being a know-it-all.	...being teachable and correctable.
...being insecure	...being secure.

I was prideful and insecure about what I was going to share. When I decided to be humble, secure, and content I could preach, prophesy, and pray for the sick in a relaxed and peaceful manner. God's power works best when we are at peace and not concerned about performing a show. True prophets will not focus on making themselves great, but will make Jesus greater as did John the Baptist.

We don't have to carry the pressure for people to be healed or God to speak to them on our shoulders because it is God's work. All we must do is be obedient to Him and love His people the way He loves us.

This attitude makes prophetic ministry healthy and something I desire to continue doing for a long time. My goal is to become a very old minister who has always been faithful to his wife, never stolen any money, and is still humbly praying for the sick, teaching, preaching, and prophesying. I pray that by the grace of God, I will be instrumental in the formation of thousands of new prophets in the decades to come. But I will reach this goal only if I manage to remain humble.

I find myself often meditating on Edward's definition of humility so that I can remain humble—being content, being kind, friendly, and respectful even to people who are different than myself. I endeavor to remain teachable, correctable, and secure in that I hear God's voice echoing in the chambers of my heart saying, "You are my dearly beloved child, I am pleased with you."

Love, courage, and humility are three essential prerequisites of anyone who wants to have a long-lasting and effective prophetic ministry.

Two Leaders and Their Strategies to Conquer Humanity

One leader who has highly influenced me in my thinking regarding the importance of humility, love, and courage is Ignatius of Loyola. I invite you to take some time to reflect on the following story I have adapted from his *Meditation on Two Standards* from his book on *Spiritual Exercises.*[25]

An enormous war is raging for all of humanity. On one side is Lucifer, the lord of darkness, whose name ironically means angel of light. On the other side is Jesus Christ, calling His troops to overcome evil with good (see Rom. 12:21). Let us examine the strategies of these two generals and their armies.

Lucifer

Imagine the throne of the evil one with smoke coming out and a huge company of demons with their hooks, chains, lances, and weapons of torture as they listen to their leader at his capital in Babylon. Hear the demons squeal and squeak in delight as they hear their leader describe their strategy for the domination of humanity.

My dear military, we will continue to go forth to conquer all of humankind. Our enemies can never win against our strategy. I am assigning each one of you to different nations, cities, families, and individuals where you may all create havoc, disorder, and destruction. We will infiltrate every arena of society from the media, to education, to churches and political systems, and men's powers will be defenseless against our onslaught.

We will convince people that they do not need anyone but themselves, and in this they will become isolated and addicted so we can wreak havoc in their lives. They will fall into our deception and our strategy will lead them to be bound and blind because they cannot say no to what we have to offer. You will all continue to spin the lives of humanity in a downward spiral, which will lead to the destruction of billions and ultimately to their own self-destruction.

The first step in our strategy is to get people to live for ***riches****. If we can get them to live for material wealth and possessions, then we will begin the process of owning their hearts. Once this has taken place, then we will overwhelm them with a desire for empty* ***honor****. They will live for vanity and believe that if they can be honored, respected and loved by men, then they will be truly happy. Yet, my sweet infantry, you can continue to tear their lives, families, and cities apart as they believe the illusion that being glorified by others will bring authentic satisfaction. Then we will have them in our throes and lead them to living a life led by* ***pride****.*

Pride is the ultimate stronghold from which all other evils come from. When they are only living for themselves, yes, then every power of lust, jealousy, fear, greed, hatred, and destruction will be their lord and master. They may think that they are truly living for their own happiness and power, but we will be their masters, and there will be no need for them to believe in us or in our enemies. We will be their lords, and they will bow down to our altars while thinking that they are their own masters. I send you out to wreak havoc and destruction and bait humanity ***first with riches, second with vain glory, and finally with pride****.*

When they give in to our strategy, then they will be our peons and possessions. They will belong to us, and we can do with them whatever we want to do. Let us ride out to steal, kill, and destroy every semblance of their creator and let them believe that their lives are in their own hands.

Can you hear the chains, hooks, and weapons of the evil ones rattling and their voices squealing? Can you hear them chant the names of the nations, cities, and individuals they have been assigned to destroy? Are they mentioning your country, your city, your church, or even your name? Could they have a plan to seed your life with the illusion of living for riches, vain-glory, and pride?

Jesus Christ

On the other side, we find a humble yet very attractive Jesus Christ who is calling us all to be His apostles (sent ones); to bring His kingdom into every corner of the world. Full of compassion, tenderness, and love He begins to describe His strategy.

"Thank you for hearing the call and the heartbeat of My Father, which is reaching a hurting and dying world. We want to reach this world with My love and power. Know that our strategy is very different to the ways of this world. I am calling you out to be salt and light and build communities of radical love and service. I am calling you to wash the feet of the ones around you and love them the way that I love and serve you.

First, I am calling you to live lives of ***spiritual poverty.*** *This means that you will live as I live: in complete dependence on* *my Father. Through the help of My Spirit, you will do what I am doing and say what I am saying together with Me to the people of the world* (see John 5:19). *Your identity will not be found in what you do or what you have or even in what people think of you but in the voice of my father continually saying,* ***'You are my beloved child and I am pleased with you.'***

This will give you the strength and stability to follow Me in ***suffering.*** *In order to follow Me, you must daily deny yourself, pick up your cross and come after Me* (see Matthew 16:24). *People will ridicule you, spit on you, lie about you, and hate you. But I am calling you not to live a life led by a desire for revenge or even to be respected but by a desire to be obedient and to love.*

Are you willing to obey Me even when it is difficult and uncomfortable? Do you realize if you lose your life for Me, you will gain it? (see Matthew 16:25) *Are you willing to suffer and give up everything for Me? If so, then you are prepared to live a life of* ***humility.***

True ***humility*** *leads to a life of real satisfaction, contentment, security, learning, and love* (see Zeph. 3:12-13). *Your entire reality and value is grounded in being created and redeemed by Me. I was called both a Lion and a Lamb, and so you to must learn when to be like a lion and when to be like a lamb* (see Revelation 5:5, 6). *True humility is power under the control of My love.*

When the world sees a radical army following Me ***in spiritual poverty, suffering, and true humility****, then there will be no demon in hell that can stop us. Will you join Me in loving the poor, the rejected, the unclean, and the undesirable with My love? Will you pray and bless your enemies and forgive those who despise you the way that I forgave the ones who crucified Me? Will you conquer evil with good? Will you forget* *your rights to be offended and be an ambassador of reconciliation? Will you say, 'Jesus, my life and all that I have is not my own. It all belongs to you. My life, my money, my family, my future, my education, EVERYTHING belongs to you. It is no longer mine, but yours'?*

Out of this kind of true humility you can hear My voice and convey My love, power, peace, holiness, and every other godly virtue. I am calling you to establish communities of My followers who will show the world that My kingdom is not about rules, but about righteousness, joy, and peace in the Holy Spirit (see Romans 14:17). *It is not simply about talk, but about power* (see 1 Cor. 4:20).

You will exemplify radical generosity, love, and service in a way that the world is longing to see. Instead of taking, you will give; instead of hating, you will love. You will demonstrate that the way to authentic freedom and life is dying to yourselves to live for me.

How will you answer my call to come and follow Me ***in spiritual poverty, suffering, and humility? Will you hear my voice and speak my words to a broken and hurting world?***

These two leaders demonstrate two radically different paradigms. One promises notoriety, influence, and glory. However, it is a trap of pride and vanity that leads to being under the power of the forces of hell. The other lived a life that demonstrated the truth of His statements. He was gentle and lowly of heart, and His foot-washing humility demonstrated to His followers that our Heavenly Father works best in servants who come to Him in their weaknesses.

There can be a thrill or temptation to pride when speaking words from God and seeing miracles result from your prayers. God calls His people to love, courage, and humility because these character traits are armor against the temptations of the enemy.

I ask you the same thing Jesus does: will you show the love of Jesus courageously, pre-determined that His ministry through you is not about you, but about Him? If so, you are ready to grow in prophecy.

Chapter 3
How To Cultivate Prophetic Ministry

"A safe place should be provided within a local church for the believer to learn how to prophesy, to heal the sick and to minister in evangelism." -John Wimber[26]

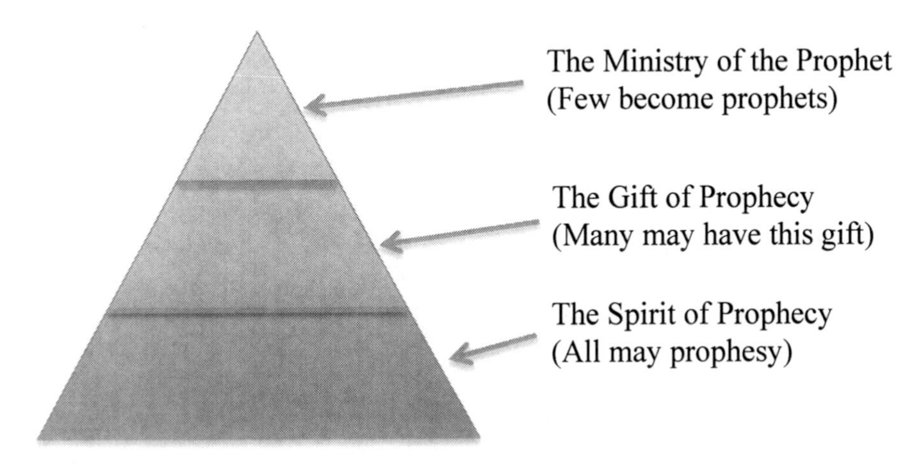

Rearing my children in the Netherlands requires them to take swimming lessons, for there are many canals they may fall into. This is a rite of passage in the Netherlands, and my older children all have their swimming diplomas. They can dive, go through underwater obstacles, and swim fearlessly at the deep end of the swimming pool. They have all completed courses in swimming, something that I never did.

I remember as a six-year-old jumping from the diving board intentionally landing on my swimming teacher. I was afraid of swimming at the deep end! I hated it and much preferred to stay at the shallow end where I could reach the bottom of the pool.

Just as swimming at the shallow end of the swimming pool is significantly different from swimming at the deep end, there are differences in prophesying at the different levels of prophetic ministry.

For our purposes, I want to define the shallow end as the Spirit of Prophecy, where everyone can jump in. I will define the middle area as the Gift of Prophecy, where many may be able prophesy, and the deep end as the Office of the Prophet, where fewer people are called and equipped to function. Let us start by examining the shallow end of the prophetic swimming pool: The *Spirit of Prophecy.*

The Spirit of Prophecy

The Spirit of Prophecy is the entry level of prophetic ministry. Revelation 19:10 says, *"Worship God! For it is the Spirit of prophecy who bears testimony to Jesus."* In the Old Testament, an example of this is in 1 Samuel 19:19-24.

> *Word came to Saul: "David is in Naioth at Ramah"; so, he sent men to capture him. But when they saw a group of prophets prophesying, with Samuel standing there as their leader, the Spirit of God came on Saul's men, and they also prophesied. Saul was told about it, and he sent more men, and they prophesied too. Saul sent men a third time, and they also prophesied. Finally, he himself left for Ramah and went to the great cistern at Seku. And he asked, "Where are Samuel and David?"*
> *"Over in Naioth at Ramah," they said.*
> *So, Saul went to Naioth at Ramah. But the Spirit of God came even on him, and he walked along prophesying until he came to Naioth. He stripped off his garments, and he too prophesied in Samuel's presence. He lay naked all that day and all that night. This is why people say, "Is Saul also among the prophets?"*

Saul and his soldiers wanted to capture David, but instead, the Spirit of God overpowered them, and they all began to prophesy.

This is a wonderful example of how even unbelievers can prophesy under a strong anointing of the Spirit of Prophecy. The Spirit of Prophecy can show them God is real and His presence can actually be felt.

Once I spoke at a youth group where no one was interested at all in prophetic ministry. Early in the evening, one woman said that she did not know if God really existed. Then I learned that three of the young men there were Muslims. Faith and expectancy for God to move was non-existent!

This all changed when I began prophesying to them. Their eyes got wide open as I started telling them one-by-one about things in their past, present, and future. For about sixty minutes, I prophesied over each of them, and I could sense the level of their faith getting higher and higher!

After that, I issued a challenge for each one of them to ask God to say something to them. To my amazement, all of them—including the agnostic woman and Muslim men—started receiving accurate words and mental pictures with symbolic meaning from God!

The highlight of the evening for me was seeing the change that took place in the woman who had said earlier that she wanted to know if God really existed. Tears ran down her face as God spoke to and through her. A few weeks later, I baptized her. Prophecy is a powerful tool to convince people that God is real.

Prophecy is a powerful tool to convince people that God is real.

The Bible says in 1 Corinthians 14:24-25: **"***But if an unbeliever or an inquirer comes in while* ***everyone is prophesying****, they are convicted of sin and are brought under judgment by all, as the secrets of their hearts are laid bare. So they will fall down and worship God, exclaiming, "****God is really among you!"*** (Emphasis added)

In no way am I advocating that non-Christians or immature, rebellious Christians regularly prophesy. Those who wish to prophesy regularly must be accountable, humble, and students of the Scriptures. All prophecies must be evaluated and tested by Scripture. If they contradict Scripture, do not accept them. This is important especially when the Spirit of Prophecy is strong, because *anyone* with a high level of faith can potentially prophesy. It is important to be able to encourage, instruct, and correct people when necessary when the Spirit of Prophecy is present.

This Spirit of Prophecy, the shallow end of the prophetic swimming pool, takes place under a special set of circumstances:

1) During the time of worship when the Spirit of God is very tangible and all may easily receive a message from God

2) When people come into a group of prophets or are challenged by a minister to jump in and start prophesying[27]

At this level, all prophesying should be focused on *"strengthening, encouragement and comforting"* one another and *not* foretelling the future (see 1 Corinthians 14:3). Prophetic messages at this level should not be corrective or directional and should aim at encouraging people and making the love of God tangible.

Avoid prophesying about births, marriages, healings, or deaths in the shallow end. God does speak about these things, but it involves a higher level of responsibility, which is better left for the more experienced ministers or prophets. If God does reveal something regarding one of those issues, ask Him if you should say anything, and, if so, when and to whom. If in doubt, refer to a mature leader as to what to say or do regarding such a word. If you do make a mistake in any of these areas, apologize!

For example, if God reveals that someone is going to marry someone else, you could simply write it in a sealed and dated envelope, and on the day of the wedding you can give it to the newly married couple.

Regarding healing, do pray for healing. However, be careful when saying "God says you are going to be healed or you will have a baby." Unnecessary damage can be done by people saying, " God is going to heal you" or " God says, you are going to get pregnant" and it does not happen. If a couple wants to have a baby, I never prophesy that they are going to have a baby. Instead, I pray that they will be able to get pregnant. God can and does speak regarding these issues, but this kind of prophetic word carries a high level of risk and responsibility.

God once told Pastor Robert Morris that his daughter was pregnant before she knew about it. She was not supposed to be able to get pregnant. He told her that she was pregnant and immediately she started taking medicine in case she was pregnant. Four weeks later the doctors told her she was pregnant and because she had taken that medicine at that time she had probably saved her baby's life. [28] God does speak about these things, but we must be wise in what we do with that information.

Prophetic ministry has gotten a black eye in the past because people misuse a "word from God" to manipulate people and force them to do things they do not necessarily desire. Having guidelines and accountability to other ministers and prophets helps protect and cultivate a healthy, life-giving prophetic culture.

Everyone probably will make mistakes when growing in prophetic ministry. This is why it is important that *all* prophetic words be tested and evaluated no matter who is prophesying (see 1 Thess. 5:19-22). In his book, *Growing in the Prophetic,* Mike Bickle has a diagram which helps illustrate this point.[29]

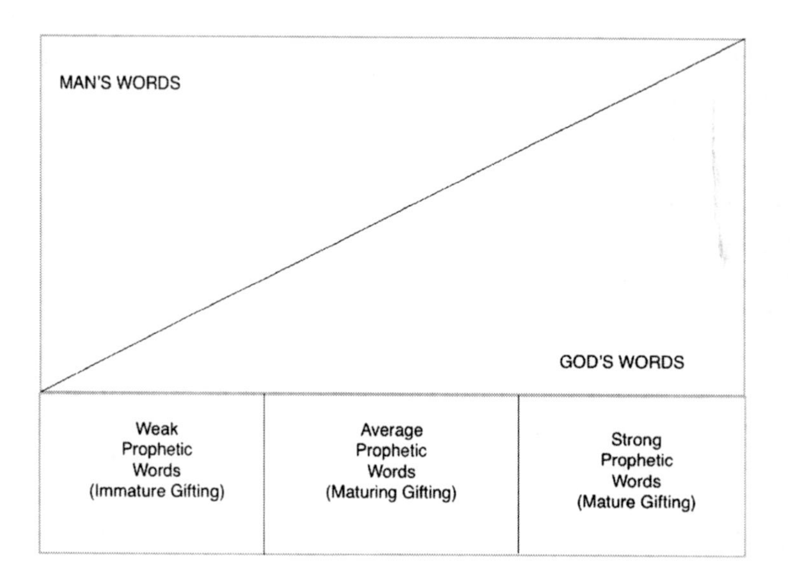

On the left side of the diagram the simplest form of prophetic ministry is illustrated. There, a high percentage of what is said may simply be coming from a person's own heart mixed in with words that come from God as well. As a person grows in prophetic ministry and intimacy with God, the percentage of accurate words from God continues to increase and words which are simply from their own heart decreases. Nevertheless, even the most experienced prophet, can deliver a prophetic word that comes from their own heart and not from God's heart. This is why testing words and giving feedback to those who desire to grow in prophetic ministry is so vital.

One Saturday morning, one of my children, who shall remain nameless, came to me and said, "Papa, mama wants you to go to the bakery and buy croissants and warm bread for breakfast."

I immediately knew that these were the words that came from my wife, Femke. She likes to have bread from the bakery on Saturday mornings. My child proceeded to say, "And she says that she wants there to be cheese croissants and chocolate croissants."

Then I realized that my child was misusing the name of my wife to get what my child desired. My child wanted the cheese and the chocolate croissants, but I know that my wife never wants that.

In the same way, we must listen to words given to us and discern what is coming from God's heart and what can be simply coming from that own person's desire or opinion. Discernment and wisdom is necessary when evaluating a prophetic word.

If we have a personal relationship with God, we will have a good idea when a word truly comes from Him and not from someone's own heart. Just like I know Femke well enough to recognize her words in my children's words, so we can know God well enough to recognize His words in the words of his children. This does require a level of maturity and responsibility for those who are receiving prophetic ministry to properly evaluate a prophetic message.

> We can know God well enough to recognize His words in the words of his children.

Shawn Bolz in his book *Translating God* tells of seasoned and experienced prophets who nearly always prophesy accurately, but when they prophesied about certain subjects their words were inaccurate. This had to do with those prophets' own need for inner-healing or own opinions.

People can mistake things that simply come from their own hearts and are not necessarily coming from God's heart. This highlights the need for accountability and transparency for *everyone* who ministers God's Word.

One example that Bolz gives is his mentor, Bob Jones, rejecting the idea that Bolz should be in Los Angeles, California. Apparently, Jones had a prejudice against Los Angeles. Bolz had to tell his mentor that though he respected his advice and influence, he did not agree with his opinion. He felt God's calling him to Los Angeles. Since then, Bolz has planted and is pastoring a thriving church in the city of Los Angeles.

In the early 1990's, Michelle McLain prophesied over one of her friends dying of sickle cell anemia, "*You shall not die but live and declare the works of the Lord* (Psalm 118:17)." Her friend died the next week. McLain was devastated and had to repent for prophesying something which came from her own heart, but not from God's mouth.[30] Once more, this highlights the need to listen well to God. If, and when, we make a mistake, we must be ready to humbly apologize and learn from our mistakes.

Whenever I minister prophetically, I try to use an evaluation form where people can give me feedback about prophetic ministry they have received from me or one of my teams. In Holland, I commonly get a 60-100% accuracy rate on the prophetic words that I give to people. I would love to say that I am always 100% accurate in everything I say, but then there would be no need to test and evaluate what is being said. It also does great in always keeping me humble. It forces me to also be sensitive to what God is saying now and not just base what I have done or said in the past.

God told Moses once to strike a rock and that water would come out of it (see Exodus 17:6). He obeyed God, and it happened just as God said. Yet at another time, God said to speak to a rock and water would come out of it. Moses disobeyed, however; he did what he had previously done, and hit the rock two times (see Numbers 20:6-12).

There is a danger when we fall back into using methods that have previously worked but are not necessarily how God wants to work at that moment. We must always be sensitive, listening to God, and ready to accept His guidance.

Sometimes when using words of knowledge on the streets, I may get accurate words for two or three individuals in a row and be totally off on the fourth person. This could be for several reasons, but one of them can be because I was simply doing what worked the previous time without being sensitive to what God was saying at that moment. Prophecy is about being sensitive to Jesus and to the people we are speaking to. There is not one approach or formula that is always good for everybody.

A great example of this is how Jesus speaks to Mary and Martha in two totally different ways after their brother, Lazarus, died. Both sisters said the same words to Jesus: *"Lord, if only you had been here, my brother would not have died" (John 11:21, 32).* Jesus answered Martha with words, and He answered Mary by simply weeping with her (see John 11:24-26, 35).

Just as I talk to my children in a way that is correct for their age and character, so God speaks to his children in ways that they can understand. Our job as ones who prophesy is to listen well to God and lovingly and carefully find the best way to speak His words so that people can receive it.

> Our job as ones who prophesy is to listen well to God and lovingly and carefully find the best way to speak His words so that people can receive it.

Our main goal as prophetic ministers should not be simply to become more accurate but to love Jesus and to love people better. Our goal is the same as that of the Prophet John the Baptist—to make Jesus greater (see John 3:30).

All the gifts of the Spirit are about love, and when we fail in this, we have missed the whole point.

> All the gifts of the Spirit are about love, and when we fail in this, we have missed the whole point.

In his book, *School of the Prophets,* Kris Valloton tells a story that illustrates this.[31] One Sunday in 1998, the new pastor at his home church asked the people to go to those they needed to ask for forgiveness for things they had said or done in the past. To Valloton's horror, a long line of people came up to him to tell him about incidents when he had given them an accurate prophetic word that had ended up causing them problems because he delivered them in an unloving fashion. He realized that day that giving an accurate word in an unloving and ungracious spirit can be devastating. It does not accomplish God's will.

In 2010, after I felt insulted by a leader, I turned to him and rebuked him for his *"lack of faith and vision."* Later that year, I had to call him and apologize for disrespecting him and his ministry. He graciously accepted my apology, and I learned an important lesson—never use the authority and power that comes with prophetic ministry when angry or offended by someone. That is when prophetic ministry can stop being life-giving and do damage. New Testament prophetic ministry is primarily for encouraging, strengthening, and comforting people and never for bullying.

One woman told me about a traumatic experience when people declared over her in front of an entire church that she was a failure in life and that she would never succeed. Those people spoke a curse over her life. I immediately broke the power of those words over her life and prayed God's blessings over her. Life and death are in the power of our tongue and prophecy should not be used to curse someone (see Prov. 18:21).

One woman came to Kenneth E. Hagin and complained about a group spending a lot of time prophesying over each other and only telling her bad things. They said her mom was going to die in six months. Eighteen months later, she was still alive. They also said her unbelieving husband was going to leave her. This was also something she did not want. Hagin immediately released her from the negative words spoken over her.[32]

If someone does this, then it is most likely not the Holy Spirit leading them, but it is their own spirit or possibly an evil spirit. We must use God's words to give life otherwise we could fall into "charismatic witchcraft."

Charismatic Witchcraft: The Dark Side of Prophetic Ministry

In 1 Samuel 18:10-11, we find a very odd story. Saul is prophesying in his house when an evil spirit comes upon him. He takes his spear and tries to murder David by pinning him against a wall. Saul had learned how to prophesy by being around Samuel and a group of prophets. However, he was prophesying from a different spirit than the Holy Spirit. When this happens, the results can be deadly.

At times, I have encountered resistance to the prophetic ministry from people who have experienced something called "charismatic witchcraft." That is where people who do not understand the Gospel or confuse New Testament prophecy with Old Testament prophecy speak judgment or even curses on people or congregations. These people are using their gift to manipulate, control, or destroy people. The fruit of such a ministry can be highly destructive, and it is distinctly ungodly.

I have spoken to people who have been victims of such a "ministry," and it is evil and should never be allowed. When people misuse God's name to try to control and manipulate people, it becomes *witchcraft*.

When someone says, "God says" to promote their own political, social, personal or church agenda, they may be shutting down all discussion. People should be free to share what they feel God is saying, but there should also be room for discussion and feedback to see if God is speaking to other people in the same line. Every prophetic word must be tested (see 1 Cor. 14:29).

Witchcraft is not a woman with a long nose and a pointy hat riding a broomstick. It is trying to intimidate, manipulate, and control others. Misusing a word from God can do this.

Paul writes to the believers in Galatia saying, *"You foolish Galatians! Who has bewitched you?"* (Gal. 3:1). The people bewitching the gentile believers were Jewish believers trying to force them to be circumcised to be saved. This was contrary to the spirit and message of Jesus that Paul had preached to the Galatians.

We must test every prophetic word and discern what spirit is motivating the person who is speaking. As John the beloved wrote, *"Dear friends, do not believe every spirit, but test the spirits to see whether they are from God, because many false prophets have gone out into the world"* (1 John 4:1).

Jesus warns of false prophets when He says, "*Watch out for false prophets. They come to you in sheep's clothing, but inwardly they are ferocious wolves. By their fruit you will recognize them"* (Matthew 7:15-16).

I have had some experiences dealing with false prophets who are wolves in sheep's clothing. This type of people will not submit to any kind of leadership and are full of rebellion and misuse God's name to promote their own agenda. They may use smooth talk and flattery to deceive the minds of gullible people (see Romans 16:17-18). Such people will claim that they can experience God's leading and claim that anyone who disagrees is not hearing God. Pride, arrogance, and insecurity hide behind their mask of "super-spirituality," and they can be very unstable and dangerous. *Every prophetic word must be tested*!

Every prophetic word must be tested!

However, we are not to despise prophecy, nor are we to discourage those who are trying to grow in hearing God's voice. We must evaluate it and judge every prophetic word, holding on to what is good and rejecting every kind of evil (see 1 Thessalonians 5:19-22). It is foolish to blindly accept a prophetic word without testing it first. If someone gives you a word from God, test it. Realize that even the disciples, Peter, James, and John, had moments in their ministry when they were not following the Holy Spirit and had to be rebuked by Jesus (see Matthew 16:23; Luke 9:54, 55). If they could make mistakes, so can we!

Fortunately, I have come across relatively few false prophets in my life and have enjoyed helping many Christians grow in the prophetic. For example, a woman who began to prophesy felt all the emotions of people she was prophesying to and told them things about themselves which were neither strengthening, encouraging, or comforting. I had to gently correct and encourage her. Now I am happy to see her flourish in her gift. She is not only operating in prophetic ministry biblically, she is activating others to do the same. No matter how much experience a person may have, there is always room for learning more and growing deeper in prophetic ministry.

Discernment of Spirits Helps Protect Us From Evil Spirits

"Dear friends, do not believe every spirit, but test the spirits to see whether they are from God, because many false prophets have gone out into the world." 1 John 4:1

One day I was sitting next to a swimming pool watching my children when I heard a voice inside of me saying, "I can give you a lot of power."

Immediately I recognized by the texture of the voice this was not the voice of Jesus, but demonic. I rejected this offer and commanded it to leave. Five minutes later, my wife pulled my then three-year old son out of the swimming pool face down. She pulled him out just before he could have suffered permanent brain damage or worse. I nearly lost one of my beloved children and this *could have had* something to do with a demonic visitation, and not just because my son decided to take his floaters off and try to swim. Jesus was visited by the devil, and we should not be surprised if the enemy tries to tempt us or deceive us in order to destroy us.

Kenneth E. Hagin as a young believer had a demonic encounter in his bedroom. He woke up and felt a presence in his room that began quoting scripture to him. It said, "What is your life? It is even a vapor that appeareth for a time, and then vanisheth away." The voice paused and then said, "and today thou shalt surely die" (James 4:14; Is. 38:1). [33]

The young Hagin thought this was the voice of God and then prepared himself to die. He remained in his chair from 8:30 until 14:30 waiting to die. But then God's voice began to speak repeatedly and gently in his heart, "With long life will I satisfy him, and shew him my salvation" (Psalm 91:16). He then realized that the first voice was not God, but from the devil.

I have seen people make mistakes because they confuse God's voice with either their own or Satan's. This has led them to make very bad decision.

A friend of mine, before becoming a Christian, was searching how to distinguish the voice of God from other voices he experienced. One of the keys that helped him was to ask any voice he experienced if Jesus was Lord (see 1 John 4:1-3). This key was crucial for him to discern if what he felt was from God or not.

We can also distinguish God's voice from any other voice by the texture of the voice. In John 10:4-5, Jesus is described as a shepherd who leads his sheep by his voice. If God speaks to you, it will not create fear, doubt, worry, or confusion. He will not control, manipulate, or damage you or others. He does not beat His sheep to go somewhere, but walks ahead of us and calls us by our names.

What we experience must also line up with Scripture. It is more important than our experiences. As Hagin said, "We are not to seek or follow voices and signs, we should follow the Word of God through Scripture."[34]

Also, do not confuse the power of the Holy Spirit with psychics and other paranormal activity that comes from the occult. Believers should avoid tarot cards, horoscopes, reiki, ouija board, etc. Anything that does not come from Jesus Christ and agree with Scripture can be extremely dangerous.

The devil is also good at quoting Scripture (see Luke 4:10-12). This is why we must be students of Scripture and understand the heart of God. Throughout the Bible, people misuse God's name to promote their own agenda (see 2 Kings 18:25). Do not allow people to manipulate or control you when they misuse the name of God or Scripture. Stay close to Jesus, and stay away from all forms of witchcraft, magic, horoscopes, and occult practices.

The Gift of Prophecy: A Deeper Level of Prophetic Ministry

The Gift of Prophecy is one of the nine gifts of the Holy Spirit that the Apostle Paul describes in 1 Corinthians 12:4-11. Those who realize that they have this gift may use it anywhere and everywhere by faith.

For me, it makes little difference if I am at a church, a supermarket, a street corner, a business office, a brothel, or even at a psychic fair: by faith I can prophesy because I know that God is always speaking. Romans 12:6 says, *"If God has given you the ability to prophesy, then prophesy whenever you can -- as often as your faith is strong enough to receive a message from God"* (TLB).

This means that I always try to keep my faith strong and my "spiritual antennas" ready, so that at any moment I can receive and deliver a message from God.

When I first started moving in the prophetic in 2010, I inquired of a prophet in Tulsa how to do prophetic evangelism. I asked her, "Do I ask for a clue? Do I go treasure hunting?"

She replied, "No, you just have the guts to walk up to someone and tell them what God wants to tell them."

That night I went to a drug store and two gas stations where I walked up to strangers and told them what God wanted to tell them. It was and remains something which takes a lot of courage, but I find I get a huge rush when I get to deliver an accurate word of knowledge, a prophetic word, or a healing to an absolute stranger at a mall, supermarket, or gas station.

In October of 2016, I took a team from a church in Fresno, California, to the streets to do "power evangelism." Outside one barbershop a group of men were astonished that I could tell them details about their lives without ever having met them. This led to several of them receiving a physical healing - when I prayed for them. The owner of the barbershop had severe pain in her back, hands, and knees. When I prayed for her she was completely healed. Soon others started coming to the barbershop asking for prayer and being healed.[35] In those cases, I did not have to wait for a special word, feeling, or sensation to minister to these individuals. I just stepped out by faith and began prophesying.

I believe God wants to heal and speak to people—everywhere and all the time. My job is to lovingly, humbly, and courageously approach people and share the love of God with them. The challenge is finding ways to communicate our message in a way people can receive what we have to offer. People may reject my offer of prayer, yet I continue to see God touching and even healing people in some of the most unexpected places through prayer

Since 2016, my wife and I have ministered to prostitutes who work in the Red-Light District of Amsterdam. We are always amazed how the atmosphere of a brothel can change when we begin to minister to these dear individuals. Every time we visit them, our goal is to let them know that God loves them and they are special to Him.

We were confirmed in this outreach to prostitutes by a significant encounter with Riana, a Colombian woman in Munich, Germany. In July of 2016, I was getting a few snacks at a supermarket when I heard a woman talking Spanish. I realized that she was a Christian and immediately began speaking prophetically to her. She was amazed and told me that everything I said was totally correct. That encounter was followed by two evenings of ministry to her household and a large group of Latin American friends she invited over. That was very significant, but most significant was what she told me when she heard of our outreach to prostitutes in Amsterdam.

"Now I understand why God wanted me to meet you guys," she said. "When I was seventeen years old, I came to Europe thinking that I was going to work as a nanny taking care of children. When I came here, I was forced into prostitution. Every night my pimp would come and demand his share of the money I had brought in that day. I became so hopeless that I became addicted to drugs to still the pain and the hopelessness I felt. However, there were Christians who regularly visited me and showed me that God loved me. They showed me love. They showed me Jesus, and I was eventually able to get out of that life of prostitution."

This illustrates once again how that the gift of prophecy is never about *"just prophesying"* but ultimately is about sharing the love of Jesus with others so that they can find true freedom.

The Office of the Prophet

"So Christ himself gave the apostles, the prophets, the evangelists, the pastors and teachers, to equip his people for works of service, so that the body of Christ may be built up..." (Ephesian 4:11-12a)

"Surely the Lord God does nothing, unless He reveals His secret to His servants the prophets." (Amos 3:7-8)

The Office of the Prophet is one of the five ministry gifts Christ has given to the Church to equip all believers to do the work of the ministry and to see them develop lives of stability and maturity (see Ephesians 4:11-14). Prophets work together with apostles, pastors, evangelists and teachers and should never work alone. Just as teachers teach people to teach and evangelists help people to evangelize, so prophets help God's people learn how to discern God's voice and speak His words. The primary ministry gifts that the Church in the Western world focuses on are those of the teacher and the pastor. Therefore, there are many outstanding teachers and pastors, but there are relatively few prophets.

Prophets work together with apostles, pastors, evangelists and teachers and should never work alone.

In 2003, Dr. Doug Beacham, the current bishop of my church (International Pentecostal Holiness Church), published a book called *Rediscovering the Role of the Apostles and Prophets.*[36] In it he opened the discussion of what modern day apostles and prophets look like according to Scripture. In January of 2010, Dr. Ron Carpenter Sr., who was then the bishop, announced on a webcast that the I.P.H.C. is an apostolic and prophetic church. The I.P.H.C has embraced the roles of apostles and prophets in the contemporary church.[37] This was a confirmation for me to continue pursuing growth in prophetic ministry.

In 2009, I started searching for true prophets. God led me to two of them: one in Amsterdam and one in Chicago. Due to their help, I now find myself teaching and training people to operate in the prophetic as well as identifying and mentoring budding prophets. It is a lot of fun to see people glow when they are released to prophesy. Many times I have heard people say things like, "I feel like you gave me a new coat and released me to do things which I have been made for...I just did not know they were possible."

We need prophets. Prophets are a powerful and necessary gift to the Body of Christ. Prophets can help bring about real changes, including miracles and spiritual breakthroughs, to individuals, churches, whole communities, and even nations.

Experienced and skilled prophets are not limited to strengthening, encouraging, and comforting people, but may also operate in other areas such as: giving of guidance, correction, healing, creative miracles, prophetic worship, spiritual warfare, etc. Just as there are different kinds of teachers and pastors, thereto are different kinds of prophets with different styles and assignments.

A prophet should never usurp the authority of a pastor or local church leaders, but coordinate with them to edify the church.[38] Whenever I am ministering in a church, I make it clear that I am under the authority of the leaders of that ministry. They have the right to give me feedback and correct me. A prophet's authority in a church can only be granted voluntarily by its leadership and not usurped. Ministers should never *compete* with each other, but rather *complete* each other.

True prophets build people up, enable healing to take place, and truly love people. In Ezekiel 13:5, we read a charge against false prophets: "You *have not gone up to the breaches in the wall to repair it for the people of Israel so that it will stand firm in the battle on the day of the Lord.*"

Prophets are people who pray for others intensely. When a warrior stood in a breach in a city's defensive wall, they were saying to the enemy forces, "You will only come into my city over my dead body." This is a role of the prophet: they stand in the gap and defend against the enemy.

Prophets care for their communities, churches, and cities. True prophets build up communities to create places where people can find safety, healing, and strength to go through the difficulties of life. The prophetic ministry is all about building people up (see 1 Cor. 14:4-5).

Prophets help God's people to achieve things they thought impossible. For example, Haggai and Zechariah motivated the Hebrews to rebuild the temple at a time when they thought it would be impossible (see Ezra 5:1-2). Moses led the Israelites through the Red Sea (see Exodus 14:21). Jesus fed thousands of people with a few pieces of fish and bread and raised others from the dead (see John 6:1-14 and Mark 16:6).

I was eleven years old the first time I was aware of meeting a prophet. He simply told me, "God really loves you so much." For the next twenty-four hours, I felt like I was in the hand of God, and I began seeing mental pictures (visions) during times of prayer and worship.

For prophets, prayer is a way of life. The Dutch Prophet Wim Kok has five children, yet often when I call him he is praying. For him, worshipping God and praying for people is his favorite activity. I will never forget the time he kept waking me up every night during a trip we went on to Kiev. He was softly praying to God all night long. For him, prayer is the *ultimate pleasure in life*. That is also why God can trust His prophets with His secrets, because they really are His friends (see Amos 3:7).

Growing up I watched prophets make significant breakthroughs in the churches we helped start in the United States. The few prophets we knew had a significant impact in our lives and ministries. Nearly all of them were "self-made" prophets. They were people who spent hours at a time praying and had regular times of fasting. The way they grew in prophetic ministry was "tarrying" or spending time basking in God's presence. This is vital and important, but prophets can also be mentored and trained to accelerate this growth process. However, this training process does not substitute for spending quality time in prayer.

Graham Cooke, in his book, *Developing Your Prophetic Gifting,* states that it normally takes an individual around twenty years to become mature as a prophet, but that this time can be reduced to twelve years if they receive prophetic mentoring and training.[39] That is why establishing Schools of Prophecy and traveling around with prophetic ministry teams is such a wonderful way to cultivate budding prophets and prophetic ministers.

Prophets are also "normal" people of flesh and blood. As anybody else, they have their own imperfections. A prophet should never be placed on a pedestal as being perfect. This will lead to disappointment. Neither the prophets in the Bible nor present day prophets are infallible. Prophets have need of friends who care about them as individuals and not simply because of God's calling on their lives.

Whenever I travel, I endeavor to take a team with me and identify budding prophets in different cities of the world. I also intentionally nurture and cultivate relationships with developing and seasoned prophets. This is an intentional and strategic way of mentoring a new generation of prophetic ministers and prophets as well as growing personally. Many people who feel such a calling on their lives do not know where they can go for this kind of help and mentoring. When I began, I found few resources that could aid the development of The Ministry of the Prophet It is my prayer this book becomes such a resource to many.

The prophets Samuel, Elijah, and Elisha all raised up schools of prophets to establish a new generation of prophets for their day. We should do the same. It is one of my great joys to see communities of prophets growing up and excelling in prophetic ministry.

Cultivating the Prophetic Intentionally

As I've mentioned, every believer can be potentially activated to prophesy at the lowest level of the prophetic swimming pool (the Spirit of Prophecy). During this process, certain individual's gifts will ignite. It will become apparent they have a prophetic gift. As people continue to exercise this gift and prophesy, it will become obvious to the local church if, and when a person is called to be a prophet. If they are called to be a prophet, it will be recognizable by the fruit of their lives and ministry (see Matt. 7:17-20).

There is plenty of teaching available on how to become a pastor, teacher, and even an evangelist, but there is relatively little regarding this very important ministry of the prophet. I was first introduced to a school for training people in prophecy in 2009. Using such a school can be part of an intentional plan to cultivate a new generation of prophets and prophetic ministers.

In 2014, I trained a dozen Bible students in the prophetic ministry to prophesy at a youth conference in Pennsylvania. On the first day of training, many of the students were reticent or even afraid to prophesy. However, by the third day of training, everybody was prophesying without hesitation. During our eight-hour ride from Maine to Pennsylvania, the students started passing their cell phones to others in the van and practiced prophesying to people they did not know. It was fun and amazing how many people on the other end of the phone confirmed (sometimes with tears) how God indeed was speaking to them through these young people. It is so much fun seeing people accurately and scripturally prophesying!

The hard part is seeing them years later and learning that they stopped doing it once they stopped spending time with a prophetic mentor. Growing in prophecy and the gifts of the Holy Spirit is like learning a new language: *If you don't use it, you may lose it!*

> Growing in prophecy and the gifts of the Holy Spirit is like learning a new language: *If you don't use it, you may lose it!*

At least once a month in our church in Amsterdam, we have a prophetic evening where, after a short teaching, everyone gets to prophesy. We are intentional about cultivating a prophetic culture where it is not only the preachers who hear God's voice but all of God's children—including literal children.

Many mornings I tell my children a Bible story or read a Scripture. Then we take thirty seconds to be quiet and ask God to give us a picture. Often the pictures they tell me about are simply their own imaginations, but sometimes I recognize God truly speaking through something that they see.

One day, my son saw a roller coaster and said he felt like God was speaking about how important it is for people to help children play who don't have an opportunity to play. He did not know that later that day I would meet with the leaders of a ministry that facilitates fairs where poor children in Africa can play on large play grounds. I know this was confirmation that the same Holy Spirit who directed that meeting was speaking to my children and they were learning to hear Him.

A Dutch television show interviewed my daughter and asked her if she has ever experienced God. She told them about a healing she saw when she prayed for a woman's foot. She also told them how her daddy asks her to pray and prophecy over people regularly. She gives people pictures from Jesus. Though she does not know what they always mean, her daddy helps her find a meaning for the things she sees.

Our children find prophecy and healing to be the most natural thing in the world—because it *is*. Intentionally cultivating the ability to hear God's voice and speak for Him is something in which everyone who is a child of God can continually grow. If it were not so, then Paul would not have written to *"eagerly desire gifts of the Spirit, especially prophecy"* (1 Cor. 14:1). We can intentionally cultivate the ability to hear God's voice and speak His word. We all can grow in prophecy, no matter our age.

Chapter 4
How to Hear God's Voice

"Whether you turn to the right or to the left, your ears will hear a voice behind you, saying, 'This is the way; walk in it.'" (Isaiah 30:21)

In 2010, I sat across a prophet and asked him, "How can I learn to prophesy?"

He looked at me and said, "The same Holy Spirit I have, you have too. Just do it!"

I believed him, and that was the beginning of me regularly prophesying and using the gifts of the Holy Spirit. Someone asked me once if God always spoke to me, to which I said, "Yes, but the problem is that I am not always listening." This is true for many of us: God is always speaking, but how often are we really listening?

God can speak to us in many ways. He can speak to us through Scripture, pictures, nature, circumstances, good advice, dreams, the church, common sense, our own desires, etc. Our difficulty is not in hearing God's voice, but recognizing Him when He is speaking to us. Being able to differentiate what God is saying and what simply comes from our own heart, someone else's heart, or even from the enemy is the challenge facing everyone who wants to grow in hearing God's voice.

An important key to hearing God's voice and discerning what is truly from Him is by knowing Scripture. As the two disciples on the Emmaus road walked with Jesus, unaware that it was Him, so Jesus is still walking with us and speaking to us through the Scriptures (see Luke 24:13-35). God's primary modus operandi for speaking to us and warming our hearts by His Spirit remains through the Bible, and it is the standard by which all gifts and prophetic words from God can be judged.

God Speaks through Scriptures[40]

"My son, pay attention to what I say; turn your ear to my words." (Prov. 4:20)

Quoting Scripture is one of the best ways to pray and to prophesy. Scripture is the Word of God. When we begin to apply His Word to the lives of others while listening to His voice, amazing things can take place.

Quoting Scripture is one of the best ways to pray and to prophesy.

(Prophetic and healing ministry can be strong at Psychic Fairs)

I have a fun area of ministry that has produced amazing results. I like to minister at psychic fairs. I bring about forty to fifty Scripture cards, printed face down, on my table. I am continually amazed at how often God speaks to people directly when they randomly pick a Scripture card. Scripture always serves as a diving board from which I can speak into people's lives.

One little girl came to my table and told me she wanted to know her future. I told her to pick a card and she randomly got Jeremiah 29:11. *"For I know the plans I have for you," declares the Lord, "plans to prosper you and not to harm you, plans to give you hope and a future."*

I told her, "See, God knows your future, and He wants you to get to know Him through Jesus." I then got to pray with her and her mother to ask Jesus to come into their lives. The Word of God is living and active, and when people begin to believe it and apply it to their lives, things can happen (see Hebrews 4:12).

God speaks to me every day when I read, meditate, and pray the Bible. I can speak into people's life with a high degree of authority and confidence when I begin to speak Scripture over them. This can be as simple as saying something like this:

The Lord says I am your Shepherd and I will take care of you. I love you with an everlasting love. I want you to be of good courage because I will never leave you nor forsake you. Do not fear and do not worry for I am with you and I will care for you. As the heavens are higher than the earth, so great is my love for you (see Psalm 23:1; Jer. 31:3; Deut. 31:6; Matt. 6:34; Psalm 103:11).

Do not ever underestimate the impact a powerful Scripture, a worship song, or a Bible story can have on somebody's life. This is why I fill myself up with Scripture; so when I pray for someone the Holy Spirit can direct my prayer and I may pray exactly what they need to hear (see John 14:26). (Remember that prophecy at the shallow end of the prophetic pool should be primarily strengthening, encouraging, and comforting people and not attempting to tell the future.) Using Scripture is a wonderful way to do this.

There have been times in my life when I have struggled with depression (another word for culture shock), and meditating on Scripture has been a powerful antidote for hopelessness. Something that really helped was to make a list of all the things I am because of Christ. Every day I would read this list aloud, my identity would start shifting from how I may feel to who God says that I am.

One of my relatives told me how the only way she survived dark emotional times in her life was to get away to study her Bible and pray. This is what enabled her to come out victoriously. Confessing Scripture over our lives by praying and meditating on it is a proven way to change our lives from the inside out. It helps us to get God's perspective about our lives.

We cannot base our lives on our emotions, but we *must* anchor our reality in Scripture. If our life is led by emotions, our life will be like an unstable roller coaster going up and down depending on how we are feeling (see Ephesians 4:14). We must base our identity only on the Word of God, because it does not change (see Matt. 24:35). It is as applicable today as it was the day God inspired someone to write it.

Not only does it never change, we use the Word of God to test every prophetic word. All prophetic words *must* submit to Scripture. God is not schizophrenic; He will not tell someone to lie, cheat, gossip, murder, hate, or commit adultery when His Word speaks so clearly against these things. Inspired Scripture is what we can use to prophesy and to evaluate all prophecy.

We use the Word of God to test every prophetic word.

God Speaks Through Pictures

"Do not let them [God's Words] *out of your sight."* (Proverbs 4:21a)

"Listen to my words: 'When there is a prophet among you, I, the LORD, reveal myself to them in visions, I speak to them in dreams.'" (Numbers 12:6)

"Which of them has stood in the council of the Lord to see or to hear his word?" (Jeremiah 23:18)

The Bible is full of examples of God speaking to people through dreams and visions that at first glance may not necessarily make much sense. God loves to speak to us through pictures and symbols. Just like a picture is worth a thousand words, so a dream or a vision can communicate powerfully to us. Jesus was the master of telling stories with multiple meanings.

God spoke to Abraham using the stars of the sky and the grains of sand of the seashore (see Genesis 15:5; 22:17). God is continually speaking to us through nature and things in our surroundings (see Psalm 19).

God has not stopped speaking to us through stories and pictures.

Imagine if you were sitting across from Jesus at a dinner table. He might grab the saltshaker and say, *"You are the salt of the earth"* (Matt. 5:13). He might point at birds outside and say to look at them and see how much His Father takes care of them (see Matt. 6:26).

An easy and common way that God can show us a picture is by showing us something in our imagination. If I were to say, "Imagine a pink elephant ice skating in a purple dress," you can probably see that in your mind's eye. I have learned that God often may give me a picture I can imagine that will have a relevant meaning for someone.

Unpacking that picture and explaining what God wants to say through that picture is the fine art of learning how to discern God's voice and accurately prophesy.

What makes pictures difficult is that you don't always know what is literal and what is symbolic. One day, I told a man I saw him working on an oilrig as I prayed for him, but I figured it was symbolic. He then told me that he literally worked on an oilrig. Another time I told a woman God wanted her to dance and what I did not know is that she had just quit dancing because she felt she was not good enough to dance.

I was at a church when I saw a pancake that needed to be flipped. I said, "God says it is time to flip the pancake."

That church was facing an important season of transition and change. After the service, I realized that God used the same imagery when he called Ephraim to change (see Hosea 7:8). That church did not have a literal pancake to flip nor was God calling them to open a pancake restaurant. Instead God was speaking about a time of change that had come.

This is what makes growing in prophetic ministry fun, but also tricky. Learning how to discern what God is saying to someone literally or symbolically is part of growing in prophetic ministry.

The more you prophesy, the more you will develop a special "sign language" with God. For example, many times when I feel that God is highlighting someone's nose, He is speaking of a gift of discernment. Their mouth is about a gift of speaking. Their ears, that they are good listeners. If their knees are highlighted, I feel like God is talking about their prayer life. The more that I prophesy, the more that I experience certain symbols that God uses to speak to me that often have a similar meaning. God will speak to you in a unique way so that you will understand Him.

The Prophet Wim Kok in Bunschoten works at a machine shop. It is normal for him to give me a prophetic word describing tools and machinery that he works with all day. Jesus spoke to fishermen about fishing and farmers about farming. Peter was hungry when he saw an image of animals he was to slaughter and go ahead and eat (see Acts 10:13). God will speak to you in a way that you will understand.

For those who are dog lovers, God may use a picture of a dog that would mean faithfulness, companionship, and love. For someone who is afraid of dogs, this may mean something fearful or negative. This is why it is good to be dependent on the leading of the Holy Spirit when we interpret dreams and pictures. What may mean one thing in one context to one person may mean something totally different to another.

God Speaks Through Our Feelings and Desires

"*Keep them* [God's Words] *within your heart.*" (Proverbs 4:21b)

I was a teenager when I suddenly knew I had to visit my workplace on a Friday night to talk to a colleague. When I arrived, I told her, "God says it does not matter what kind of mess you are in in, He wants to help you out."

She replied, "Boy am I in a big mess!" The next day I learned she was in the process of stealing thousands of dollars from our employer.

On another occasion, I felt I had to call a good friend of mine in Bolivia. He was asking God whether he should start a new church. My phone call lasted about sixty seconds, and in that conversation I told him, "God wants you to start a new church." That church is doing very well.[41]

When ministering prophetically, I often feel drawn to people like an invisible string pulling me in their direction. I can only describe this as knowing that I need to say or do something for this person.

One Sunday morning, the entire football team of the little city of Wewoka, Oklahoma came to the church I was speaking at. I started by picking out the quarterback of the team and speaking about how God had called him to be a leader and the influence God wanted to give him. I did not know he was the quarterback, but most of the people there did. It was a great way to kick off that service.

It is not uncommon for me to send friends on Facebook an encouraging message. Sometimes I will get a response saying something like, "How did you know to call me then or what you just sent to me is so amazing. God gave me that same Scripture yesterday in my time of prayer."

Some people I trained in Amsterdam were practicing sending encouraging voice messages to people they knew. For some reason, they called a woman they did not know very well at all. An hour later she said when they called she was about to attempt suicide. That their message literally *saved her life*. Now she knew God cared for her and she was important to Him. Never underestimate the power of an encouraging word because the power of life and death is in our words (see Proverbs 18:21)!

Words from God are Life Giving

"For they [God's words] *are life to those who find them and health to one's whole body."* (Proverbs 4:23).

Many times, people ask me how you can test if a prophetic word is from God. One of the best ways is simply how encouraging, strengthening, and comforting the word is. During my first year of living in the Netherlands, I struggled with discouragement. On more than one occasion, I had a friend send me an e-mail detailing a dream that they had or simply an encouraging prayer saying that God was working everything out for good. Those short notes and e-mails were so life giving and encouraging for me and helped me to get through that difficult time.

At a church in Tulsa, Oklahoma, a first-time guest was shocked when I gave him a true message from God. His response was, "God just spoke to me. I have never had that happen before." The next year I was overjoyed to find him and his family as faithful members of that church. Hearing God's voice is life changing.

One American student was coming briefly to Amsterdam. I told her, "God says that Europe welcomes you."

The next week she arrived in London where she was denied entry to Europe upon arrival. She was taken to a back room where they told her to wait because she did not have the right visa. As she waited, she began to take that word I had given her and said, "Europe welcomes me. I am welcome in Europe."

A few minutes later a British immigration officer came in and said, "You don't have the right visa, but we are going to allow you into England. Welcome to Europe."

Prophecy gives us life and hope. It is like a weapon that can help us to make it through the difficult times of life. Like Paul told Timothy, *"Timothy, my son, I am giving you this command in keeping with the prophecies once made about you, so that by recalling them you may fight the battle well"* (1 Timothy 1:18).

Prophetic words help us win life's tough battles.

Prophetic words help us win life's tough battles.

Rooting our identity deeply in the unchanging Word of God enables us to go through the storms of life. Just like the roots of a tree absorb all the life-giving nutrients for the rest of a tree, so all our spiritual life and nutrition is derived from remaining in Christ. Storms will come and go, but if our hearts are rooted and grounded in His love, then we are safe. We are like trees planted by streams of water that do not fear drought, but always bear fruit (see Psalm 1:3, Jeremiah 17:8).

Guard Your Heart by Giving and Forgiving

"Above all else, guard your heart, for everything you do flows from it" (Proverbs 4:23).

If you want to hear what is in a person's heart, just listen to them talk for five minutes. If you want to hear what is in your heart, listen to yourself talk and look at what you spend most of your income on.

If you want to hear what is in your heart, listen to yourself talk and look at what you spend most of your income on.

Whenever you hear someone prophesy, you will hear words that come from that person's own heart as well as from God's heart. If a person is full of love and faith, these elements will come out when they prophesy. If they are full of fear, doubt, or insecurity, those will also manifest through their words.

What you talk about and spend your money on reveals your heart's greatest desires. Wherever your treasures are, there will your heart be also (see Matt. 6:21). Are you radically generous? Are you developing the skill of giving? (see 2 Cor. 8:7) Giving to the poor and needy is like a prayer that goes up to God as a sweet smelling offering (see Acts 10:1-5). Being radically generous is incredibly important to prevent greed from getting a chokehold on our hearts and pocketbooks.

Giving not only protects our hearts, it forms us as well. We must always be on guard against the lure of illicit money, glory, or relationships. We must strive to keep our hearts pure, for Jesus promises that we will we see God when our hearts are pure (see Matthew 5:8). This enables us to be messengers for God to others.

One day I was starting to get into a pity party. I started really feeling sorry for myself, feeling that people did not value me or see me as important as I truly was. My attitude was just like the song, "Nobody loves me. Everybody hates me. I guess I am going to eat some worms."

That night God spoke to me through a dream.

In the dream I was together with a prostitute. After being with her, I was carrying her in my arms and she was pretending to be wounded. Immediately the wife of a pastor who had been caught in an immoral situation stood in front of me rebuking me, saying, "You are stupid for carrying her!" over and over.

I ditched the prostitute, and then I was given a package to deliver at the post office for $7.77. Then I woke up.

God was telling me through the dream I could not carry a wounded spirit. I could not feel sorry for myself because that would open the door for all kinds of sin and misery in my life. It feels good (for a while) to feel sorry for myself. I can commit the sin of comparing myself with others and feel bad for what I do or do not have. This is stupidity.

The number seven in the Bible can stand for perfection or maturity. God was telling me that if I refused to carry a wounded spirit, then He would be able to trust me to carry His words to others. I can never allow my heart to become bitter and wounded because that impairs His ability to use me.

Without maturity, we can be like infants—like ships on the sea, tossed back and forth by waves and blown here and there by every wind of teaching, emotion, or circumstance (see Eph. 4:14). We can become prey to Satan, whose cunning temptations are as delicious as eating a chocolate covered banana split ice cream laced with rat poison. Sin causes us to destroy others and ourselves. Sin always leads (sooner or later) to death.

Sin always leads (sooner or later) to death.

Sometimes I speak to people who tell me about things they are angry about which happened years or even decades earlier. When we do not forgive, it is like carrying a dead bird around our neck. It is rotten. It stinks. It impairs our personal growth and development.

When we do not forgive, we place an imaginary chain on the leg of the individual who hurt us, and the other end of the chain is on our neck. Every time we think of them, toxic emotions damage our hearts. This is why forgiveness, inner-healing, and resolving conflicts are extremely important for those with spiritual authority. Getting rid of any root of bitterness in our hearts is imperative because it can corrupt many (see Hebrews 12:15).

Guarding our heart is imperative to being healthy. Rooting out all bitterness and daily replacing that with God's Word is important. Fortunately, we do not have to rely on a prophet or on any one else for God to speak to us. One of the best ways that God can speak to us is by directly hearing from him by meditating and praying Scripture.

Meditating on Scripture Using the Monk's Ladder (Lectio Divina)[42]

One thousand years ago, a monk named Guigo II de Kartuizer wrote a letter to a friend explaining how he could learn to pray by meditating on Scripture. He described a process known as the monk's ladder (Scala Claustalium) or Lection Divina. Imagine it as a ladder that you can use daily to climb into God's presence and hear Him speak to you regularly.

This method unleashes the power of meditating on Scripture to hear God's voice. The entire process can be described as *Seeking, Finding, Knocking, and a Door Opening* (Luke 11:9-10). I periodically use this method, and God not only speaks to me, but continues to change my life as I use it. Here is a diagram explaining the four steps of this special ladder.

The Monk's Ladder
(Scala Claustalium)

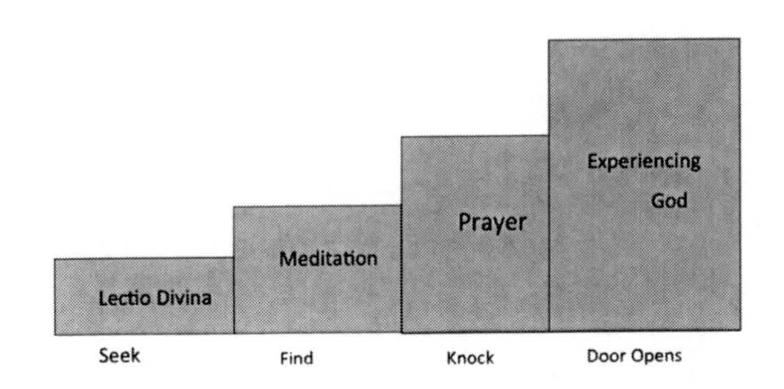

Step 1: Lectio Divina (Reading a Scripture Repeatedly)

The first step is simply reading a Scripture verse or story repeatedly, called Lectio Divina. As you read and reread a passage, one word, verse, or Scripture may jump out and grab your attention. This process is like searching for a treasure in Scripture and finding it. Once this word or words have our attention, then step two begins, which is meditation.

Step 2: Meditation

The second step is the positive version of worrying. When someone worries, they focus on negative thoughts, and those thoughts can get a life of their own. Something very small can become huge and overwhelming. Instead of worrying, focus on Scripture and allow the words of Scripture to begin to become alive. Let them become huge. Let them overwhelm you.

The digestion system of a cow is a wonderful illustration of meditation. Cows have four stomachs instead of one. When they eat, they will eat something many times over. They will chew their food, swallow it, regurgitate it, and then do this process all over again.

There are times in my life where I have spent days meditating on one Scripture or Bible story. Every time I went to reread the Scripture, I would see something I had not seen before. The Spirit of God would give me new insight or ideas regarding His words. This is a fun, dynamic, and enjoyable way of engaging God's Word in Scripture.

When reading a story, it is important to use one's imagination. Attempt to imagine tasting, touching, smelling, seeing, and feeling what is taking place in the Biblical narrative. Allow it to gain life in your thoughts and imagination. Once this has taken place, take your experience to God in prayer.

Step 3: Prayer

Whatever you are experiencing while meditating, talk to God about it. For example, if you are meditating on Psalm 23:1, you could pray things such as, "God, thank you that you are my shepherd. Thank you that I have everything that I need. Thank you for all the times you have supplied all my needs. God, will you reveal to me the times I have taken your provision for granted? God, is there anyone you want me to help by providing something they may need?"

Then remain still and see what thoughts may come to your mind. These thoughts could be simply your own, but they could also be God speaking to your heart.

Step 4: Contemplation (Experiencing God)

The word "contemplate" means to see or gaze at. God can reveal Himself to us through His Word. The most difficult part of meditation is actually taking time to get still and do it. It is not difficult, but it does require setting aside time to intentionally seek to encounter God.

> The most difficult part of meditation is actually taking time to get still and do it.

Here is a list of Scriptures that could be used to start practicing meditating on Scripture: Psalm 23, 91, 139; Ephesians 1:15-23, 3:14-21; Matthew 6:9-13; Acts 4:32-37; Jeremiah 31:33, 34; Song of Songs 8:6,7; Isaiah 6:1-8; Genesis 1:26-28; and Jeremiah 1:4-12; etc.

Using the four steps, take one or more of these Scriptures and spend an extended amount of time, fifteen minutes to an hour for example, asking God to speak to you though them. I have literally spent hundreds of hours meditating on Scriptures, and they have changed my life. Allow God to change yours as well. Meditation on Scripture is important for everyone who wants to grow in the ability to hear God's voice.

Chapter 5
How to Prophesy

"For you can all prophesy in turn so that everyone may be instructed and encouraged." 1 Cor. 14:31

I would like every one of you to speak in tongues, but I would rather have you prophesy. 1 Cor. 14:5a

In 2010, I was wide awake at 2 a.m. suffering from jet lag in Chicago. I was really missing my wife and my children. Suddenly the following thought dawned on me: "I do miss my family, and I want to be with them, but I am going to focus my thoughts on God. Yes, God, I want you. I really want to see and experience you now. I long for you."

That month changed my life as I experienced God profoundly as I set my desire on Him.

During that month, I organized two days of prayer and fasting where I taught and prophesied over people for many hours. Yet, prophesying was not the most significant; it was experiencing God's presence.

As I drove down I-44 expressway to Oklahoma City, I cranked up worship music and suddenly experienced the presence of God tangibly. Jesus was in the car with me, and I could feel Him. His presence is amazing!

Later that year, in Madill, Oklahoma, I organized another day of prayer and fasting where once again the manifest presence of God showed up. There was a divine silence that came into the church sanctuary. We knew God was in the room in a tangible way. Nobody needed to say anything, because God was there.

The most important key in growing in prophecy is seeking God's presence first and then His presents.

The most important key in growing in prophecy is seeking God's presence first and then His presents.

#1 Desire God's Presence First and then His Presents

We do not need to feel God's presence because we walk by faith and not by what we feel (2 Cor. 5:7). However, we can feel and experience God.

I once offered some tourists looking for drugs in Amsterdam some "really good stuff." I told them what I had was the best stuff possible. When I told them it was knowing Jesus, they scoffed at me, but they told me I was a good salesman. What they did not realize is that my offer was 100% true. There is no high like knowing Jesus!

In the fall of 1996, Victory Christian School was visited in a special way by the presence of God. Pastor Billy Joe Daugherty sent the high school students to the elementary classes to pray for them because we were being visited by the manifest presence of God. We had no class that day as students and teachers were being touched by the presence of God. Students fell under the power of God, wept, and prayed like never before. God visited us!

I rarely talk about these special moments because they are not common in my daily life. Most people in Europe have a hard time believing that God exists at all, let alone that He can speak to you and you can experience Him.

I have experienced God's presence and have learned to discern His presence in the less spectacular, mundane moments of life as well. I can see him in nature, my children and many other places which may seem unimportant or unspiritual. I understand David's words when he says, "One thing I ask from the Lord, this only do I seek: that I may dwell in the house of the Lord all the days of my life, to gaze on the beauty of the Lord and to seek him in his temple" (Psalm 27:4).

If we go after God because we want *stuff* from Him, we could be in danger. Simon the Sorcerer offered Peter money to have the ability to lay hands on people so they can be filled with the Holy Spirit. Peter rebuked him harshly (see Acts 8:20-25). We do not go after gifts from God first; we go after Him. As God fills our lives with His presence, the presents of His Spirit (healing, prophecy, tongues, etc.) become normal and natural.

I do desire gifts from God, but what I desire more is God Himself. His presence is the greatest present I can ever have.

#2 Keep Your House From Leaning

Downtown Amsterdam is filled with beautiful houses, many of which were built in the seventeenth or eighteenth century. Though beautiful, many of them are crooked and leaning. The soft ground in Amsterdam makes it easy for buildings to shift if they are not built on poles that go very deep into the ground. Without that foundation, those buildings will fall and lead to death and destruction.

If someone has a strong ministry gifting or anointing but lacks integrity, their leaning ministry can also lead to destruction. Do not allow your anointing to be heavier than your integrity and character.

Do not allow your anointing to be heavier than your integrity and character.

Some individuals who have had powerful ministries have appeared and disappeared like shooting stars. It is good to develop a strong anointing or gifting, but do this while being a person of integrity. Learn to keep your eyes focused on heaven with your feet solidly planted on the ground. This means being honest, paying your bills, being responsible, and treating your friends and family members with kindness.

If you want to grow in supernatural ministry, you cannot isolate yourself. Have friends who will speak the *truth* to you, no matter how much God may or may not use you. Have people in your life with whom you can be transparent and can help you when you need it.

Many people who have a strong prophetic gifting can struggle with depression and discouragement. It is vital to create accountability structures and cultivate relationships with people who can pray, listen, and advise you. I have never felt alone because I have intentionally nurtured mutually accountable relationship with great friends. They care for me because of who I am and not what I can do.

#3 Pray in the Spirit Often

Praying in the Spirit is a fantastic way to prepare for prophetic and healing ministry. It is a way of stirring up the gift of God inside of you (see 2 Tim. 1:6). It is like the butter that causes a hot frying pan to sizzle before cooking a large piece of meat. I know many prophets and healing evangelists who regularly spend many hours praying in the spirit and in their understanding (see 1 Cor. 14:15). Praying in Spirit can help the prophetic flow get going.

However, once you start prophesying do not go back and forth in tongues and in prophecy. Once you start prophesying trust that God will continue to speak through you without having to speak in tongues. Also, when appropriate, pray softly in tongues before prophesying without people hearing you do it. You don't want to unnecessarily distract people from the message you have to give to them.

#4 Relax and Don't Be Weird

Make a tight fist with your right hand and see how difficult it is to stick a finger from your left hand into that fist. Now relax and open your right-hand wide open and see how easy it is to move your left fingers into your right hand. If you want to hear God's voice clearly, *relax* and be at *rest.*

A word from God does not need to be delivered with an emotional charge or with King James English. Once you begin flowing prophetically, God's thoughts will sound just like your own thoughts. The only way to find out if they are from Him is to say what you are seeing, thinking, or feeling and then ask if what you are saying makes any sense.

Being at rest makes it easier for God to speak to us and lead us when we prophesy. Trusting God and being relaxed when prophesying is beneficial for everyone who gives and hears a prophetic word.

I am concerned about people I know who have shied away from prophecy and spiritual gifts because they saw people being flaky and weird. If God is my Father, then it is normal that He will speak to me. I do not speak to my children in King James English or get spooky with them (unless I am playing with them). So, we can talk to people conversationally and share what we feel God is saying without them even knowing it at times.

One day I walked into my son's pre-school class and saw a picture for the teacher. I wrote an encouraging note and described what I saw. The next day, I saw the note taped onto the wall where everyone could see it. I did not write, "So says the Lord..." I just encouraged her with the words I felt God wanted to speak to her. She appreciated it so much that she put it up so everyone could see what I had written. Prophetic ministry is not only for a church context, but for daily "normal" life.

#5 Flow Like A Kleenex Box

You may get one picture, word, Scripture, impression, or maybe absolutely nothing when you go to pray for a person. But as you begin to pray by faith, words may begin to flow out of your mouth like a stream of living water. When you say that one Scripture or picture, more may come. The dam may break and a prophetic flow may begin to develop.

Like a Kleenex in a Kleenex box, when you pull one out, more come. When you start speaking words of life, more can come. Often when I begin to prophesy, I do not know what I am going to say. I trust God that when I open my mouth, He will fill it (see Psalm 81:10).

I remember prophesying over a leader and hearing the words come out of my mouth, "You are known for three things."

I then thought, "Help God, what are those three things." As I continued speaking, the three things rolled out of my mouth while he nodded at me with surprise and gratefulness.

When crossing the Jordan River, the priest had to step into a deep and dangerous flooding river. It was as their feet touched the water that the river began to recede and not before (Joshua 3:13-16). God will speak through your lips when you open your mouth and not before. Prophesying takes faith in God and courage.

Nearly every time I train groups in prophetic ministry, someone freezes up and says something like: "I can't do this. This is too difficult" or, "I want it to be God and not me."

Fear will hinder us from prophesying. We want to be in control and know everything we are going to say ahead of time, so as to not make a mistake. When it comes to faith, God does not work that way. Faith is like Abraham leaving his home not knowing where he was going. Prophesying often means speaking words and not knowing what I am going to say.

> We want to be in control and know everything we are going to say ahead of time, so as to not make a mistake. When it comes to faith, God does not work that way.

One day my wife Femke was prophesying over a daughter and a mother. Femke suddenly heard songs and saw pictures from the daughter's childhood. As Femke began telling them about what she saw and heard, the two began to weep. These were cherished memories that due to traumatic events had been forgotten. Suddenly, they were back. Femke thought about one song, and more memories began to come.

Two Hebrew words for prophesying have to do with water. The first is *nataph,* which means to ooze, to distill gradually, to fall in drops, or to speak in inspiration. This is a beautiful picture of how during worship or prayer, thoughts and pictures can fall like rain into our spirits.

The second word for prophecy is *naba*. It has a sense of "bubbling or springing up, flowing, pouring out or gushing forth."[43] It is like a river of inspiration that flows from our spirits as we prophesy (see John 7:38-39 & 4:14). Often, when I first begin training people in prophetic ministry, they are reticent and insecure. As they grow, however, a strong steady prophetic flow can develop.

Sometimes when I start prophesying, people call me a machine gun prophet because I may prophesy quickly. Do not mistake a person's style or way of prophesying as the only way to prophesy. There are many styles of prophets and many ways to prophesy. The task you have is to connect to God and discern how God speaks to you and through you. This is best developed together with experienced prophets and other people learning how to prophesy.

Sometimes when I am prophesying, I feel very vulnerable. I feel like I am standing in my underwear. I don't know people, and I don't know what I should tell them. Fortunately, *I don't have to know what to say* because I prophesy from my spirit and not from my intellect. Once I start prophesying and get over the initial hurdles of fear, I may step into a prophetic river where words, pictures, and thoughts begin to flow rapidly. At that point, I recognize that God's thoughts are often my own thoughts.

The challenge remains filtering those thoughts in an appropriate manner. I must communicate those words in a way that strengthens, encourages, and comforts someone. I must articulate the message in a way they can understand. This is where developing the skill of prophesying comes into it. Just as someone can grow in their teaching ability, so they can grow in their ability to prophesy well. Part of this involves using "Prophetic Hermeneutics."

#6 Use Prophetic Hermeneutics: Revelation, Interpretation, Application

Hermeneutics is the term theologians use to explain the process of understanding Scripture. The three steps used to understand Scripture are also the same exact steps used for unpacking prophecy: Revelation, Interpretation, and Application.

Years ago, while prophesying over a woman, God began highlighting her hair to me. I had no clue what it meant, but as I began speaking about her I said, "You are a worshipper just like the woman who dried the feet of Jesus with her hair. You are a person who truly worships the Lord in Spirit and in truth." This word proved to be true about her.

A revelation can be a picture or a Scripture of which you have no idea what it means. But as you begin to unpack the revelation (Scripture, picture, dream, etc.), the Holy Spirit begins giving you the interpretation and possibly also the application.

Recently at an evening for practicing prophecy, someone walked up to me with a star from a Christmas tree saying, "I believe you are like a star which people from the East are going to seek to find Jesus."

What he did not know is I had just been asked by leaders from Eastern Europe to come and train them in Power Evangelism. Though he was thinking of a Bible story, there was a greater interpretation and immediate application for my life. He gave me the revelation, and I was able to interpret it immediately and apply it to my life.

Sometimes you may get a revelation, but not know how a person needs to interpret that or apply it. Once, I saw a woman as a mother hen with a lot of little chicks around her. I told her this and then asked her what that meant to her. She responded, "I work at a daycare, and I have been asking God if I should keep working with these children. Your picture was an answer to my prayer."

Once I was in Hungary, and I told a young woman that she was going to do prophetic ministry with me. I thought this meant she would become part of one of my prophetic ministry team members. Instead, she was the person who organized the first youth prophetic conference in Hungary. We may get a revelation, but not know how that is going to take place.

A correct revelation with the wrong interpretation or wrong application will lead to wrong results. A correct revelation and a correct interpretation with the wrong application will also lead to a frustration.

A correct revelation with the wrong interpretation or wrong application will lead to wrong results. A correct revelation and a correct interpretation with the wrong application will also lead to a frustration.

I was at a church once when I prophesied over a man that he was a leader and that God was going to use him as a king to lead many people. That man took the prophetic word and tried to split the church using the word that I gave him. The pastor, who is a good friend of mine, told me, "Matt everything that you said about him was true, but he misused that word in a wrong way and at the wrong time."

There was a gap of twenty years between Samuel anointing David to become king of Israel and when David was crowned king. David did not go out immediately to kill Saul and become king in his own strength and time; quite the opposite. David is an excellent example of someone who knew and respected God's timing.

Jesus began His ministry at the age of thirty, and it only lasted three years. All Messianic prophecies of the Old Testament were waiting to be fulfilled, and He fulfilled all of them in the proper window of time.

God is more interested in who we are than what we will do for Him. A prophetic word can be for now, a year from now, or decades from now. This is why we must not be too quick to disqualify a prophetic word we do not understand. However, we can *always* allow God to make us into the person through whom He will bring that word to pass.

In 2010, someone prophesied that God was going to use me as a leader in the United States. I immediately rejected that word because I live in the Netherlands and don't plan on living in the United States. That year, I spent four months in the USA and God did use me as a leader there!

#7: Deliver the Prophetic Pizza

When you prophesy, you are a spokesperson for God. Your job is like a pizza delivery person—you deliver what God is saying and don't force people to eat the pizza. You would be unhappy if a delivery person forced you to eat the pizza when he wanted you to. Give people space to judge the word for themselves and decide for themselves what they are or are not going to do with the message. People are responsible for their own lives and they must be able to choose what they will do or not do after receiving a prophetic word.

No one wants to eat a pizza delivered in a cold cardboard box full of holes and dirt. The box would take away from the edibility of the pizza. In the same way, present a message from God in a way that will not take away from the message itself. Be aware of appropriate dress when serving people of other cultures. Don't express your political opinions when prophesying. Use language and expressions that people will understand. Don't let your presentation get in the way of what God wants to say to a person. Avoid secondary or non-important details that can distract from a message that comes from God.

Present a message from God in a way that will not take away from the message itself.

You can go to a fancy restaurant or a cheap one to get a steak. The same piece of meat can cost a few dollars or many dollars depending on how well it is prepared and presented. Our job is to do our best to present a message from God that people can understand and digest.

Whether people accept the word or not, it is not our responsibility. But we are responsible for how we present it. The word of God is far more important than a pizza or piece of meat, so do everything possible to deliver it well.

#8: Get Feedback

As a delivery person, be open to getting feedback on how your "prophetic pizza" is understood or experienced. Don't be too excited when everything you say is 100% accurate, and don't be too discouraged if what you say is not 100% accurate. We are all learning in this, and maintaining open communication with God and those we serve is crucial for growing in the prophetic.

Kenneth Hagen was praying for a young man and suddenly he heard the words coming out of his mouth, "This is a confirmation of what I said to you at three o'clock this afternoon as you were praying in the storm cellar. You asked for a confirmation, and this is it. That was Me speaking to you."

After the service he asked him, "Were you praying down in the storm cellar at three o'clock this afternoon?"

He was. At that moment, he was asking God for a confirmation of whether he should become a preacher. He felt that God told him at that moment, "I will give you a confirmation tonight." Hagin's words were that confirmation.[44]

Often, I ask people, "Does that make sense?" This way I can learn myself, but also because I do not always know what I am saying means. Do not be concerned with how profound or impressive you come across. Some of the simplest words can have a significant meaning that you are unaware of.

One day I got the word "cookie" for a woman. I asked her, "What does that mean?" She said her grandfather's nickname was "Cookie" and he was a great man of faith. She loved him dearly, and her prayer was that his faith would pass on to her children. It was very significant to her that I began unknowingly talking about her grandfather while talking about her faith.

#9: Grow In Prophetic Ministry by Prophesying

The first time I played the guitar, it sounded horrible. Now because of lots of hours of practice, I can lead a church in praise and worship. When you first start prophesying, it may not sound very confident, perfect, or smooth. Don't let that impede you. Keep learning, studying, watching, growing and developing in prophetic ministry. I like to educate, demonstrate, activate, and help people develop in their prophetic gifting and calling. Remain loving, humble, and teachable and see how you can grow in prophecy. Learn to hear God's voice and speak His words.

#10 When Stuck, Use A Diving Board

God's thoughts about us outnumber all the grains of sand in the sea (see Psalm 139:18). He is generous and creative in speaking to us. However, there may be times when you have no clue what to say. You are totally blank. The hardest part of prophesying at times is getting started. Grab any random object, and use that as a "diving board."

Sometimes I will ask a woman to give me a random object out of her purse or use a phone number, license plate, or dream to prophesy. The most important thing is not the object I use, but the ability God has to speak to us through anything.

Two people with strong prophetic gifting accompanied me to Budapest for a conference. During a three-hour break, we walked around town and practiced prophesying over each other using the signs and things we saw during our walk. This loosened them up, and their flow became much stronger after that exercise. Prophesying takes simple, child-like faith. Using a diving board can help you if or when you get stuck.

#11 Get a Band of Brothers and Sisters

I do not like to do ministry by myself. I always like to take others with me. This is mutually beneficial, as the spiritual anointing can be contagious. I like to invest in other people's lives because it is most beneficial for myself. The best way to grow in prophecy is by prophesying and teaching others how to prophesy.

When John Wimber realized signs and wonders were following his ministry everywhere he went, he found himself facing a decision. He once told his wife Carol, "I can either get a tent and have a huge revival where I can do this by myself, or I can release it to the people, and equip them to play."[45] He chose the latter, and because of that had a much larger impact than he would have had if he did everything himself.

Prophecy and the gifts of the Holy Spirit are not just for "special anointed" people. They are for every believer. Whenever I travel, I always try to take a team of people who do the ministry with me, modeling the strategy of Jesus and the Apostle Paul. Don't hold onto ministry for yourself, but release ministry into the hands of other believers. We don't lose but *gain* authority by giving it away to others.

The best way to grow in spiritual gifts is by training others how they can use them. I celebrate and rejoice when those who I have mentored see amazing healings and miracles I have not seen yet. It is not about me, it is all about Jesus; and like Jesus I regularly say, "Everything I can do, you can do better."

If you are in a church or a place where you don't have any mentors, do not worry. I have never met most of my mentors! I have never met John Wimber, Oral Roberts, Timothy Keller, Ignatius of Loyola, T.L. Osborn, the Apostle Peter, or Apostle Paul. I have read their writings, though, and they have helped shaped my life and ministry today. Read good books and then find people with whom you can do more than just talk about what you read but *do* what they *did*. Desire to grow in spiritual gifts by not just talking about them, but by stepping out and using them.

When I first came to Amsterdam, we set up monthly men's prayer meetings where we would simply pray for each other. We would put one person in the middle and pray for whatever they needed. Often, as we prayed, God would speak through us. Some of those men are now my best friends and ministry partners. They have given me many valuable words from God on many occasions.

#12 Prophesy like Charlie Brown's Little Red-Haired Girl

I was biking with my daughter after watching a Charlie Brown film when she surprised me by saying, *"Papa, the little red-haired girl is a prophet just like you. Right, Papa?*

Everyone in *The Peanuts Movie* has the tendency to treat poor Charlie Brown badly. Lucy is constantly pulling away the football when he wants to kick it, people make fun of him and he feels like a big *loser*. But by the end of the movie, to his own amazement, the little red haired girl wants to be his pen pal.

She wants to be his pen pal because he is honest, funny, smart, sincere, and caring. She strengthens, encourages, and comforts him, leaving Charlie Brown and the viewer with a warm feeling.

My daughter equated this heart-warming experience to the meetings she has had with prophets. Prophets speak God's truth in love and bring out the best in other people. A prophet's greatest goal is not to prophesy, but to love people the same way God loves us. Focus on Jesus and loving people and prophesying can become easy and natural.

Chapter 6
Prophetic Activations[46]

"I am the LORD your God, who brought you up out of Egypt. Open wide your mouth and I will fill it." (Psalm 81:10)

"When you are brought before synagogues, rulers and authorities, do not worry about how you will defend yourselves or what you will say, for the Holy Spirit will teach you at that time what you should say." (Luke 12:11-12)

(The best way to grow in prophetic ministry is together with others.)

The best way to learn something is together with other people. This chapter contains a list of possible group activation exercises. It is important to experiment with how God may speak to and through you to others. An ideal way to do this is to have a group with one central leader who assigns the different exercises. Just like growing a muscle requires exercises, so the prophetic gift can grow in us when we exercise the gifts and stir up the fire of the Holy Spirit within us. (see 2 Tim. 1:6).

Leaders will have to find the balance in challenging people to grow outside of their comfort zones and avoid situations that freeze people up. Creating a safe learning environment where people can be challenged, encouraged, and corrected when necessary helps cultivate healthy prophetic believers. Make these exercises a "learning experience where all can grow."

It is good to briefly pray in tongues before starting each exercise; this helps participants get a prophetic flow going. If participants do not pray in tongues yet, praying in their native tongue will suffice. The leader will tell people when to start and stop praying in tongues and begin prophesying.

Prophetic Activations

- **Around the Circle** - Everyone in the circle gets a number and prophesy over the person on their right until everyone in the group has prophesied over the person next to them. When beginning, students may be afraid to speak. Encourage them to simply pray words of encouragement, strengthening, and comfort. This is the most basic form of prophetic ministry.

  This is normally the first exercise I will do with people to "warm up." Because the word prophecy holds so much weight in their mind, it can be difficult for them to speak. Encourage them to simply pray for each other. At this point, they may be simply praying for each other. That is fine. Prophecy is a natural part of prayer because when we speak to God, he will speak back to us.

- **Switch** - The group leader will say, "Switch," when people need to stop or start prophesying. If they say switch quickly, this will force participants to not think too much but simply by faith say what the Spirit of God will lead them to say. If the switch is delayed, this will challenge those prophesying to not stop prophesying but by faith ask God for more they can give. It also teaches participants to hold a word. A prophet is in control of himself and can be quiet when he or she needs to be quiet, such as when it is not their turn to speak.

One prophet who traveled with me had a difficult time with me calling "switch" while she was prophesying the first time. She wanted to give the entire message God had for a person at that moment. Fortunately, she listened to me and learned the value of being able to hold onto a word from God. Just because God may give you a word for someone does not mean you must give the entire word at that moment. Learning to hold a word and wait for the right timing to give it is important. It is also important to learn to submit to authority when they feel it is not the right moment to give a word or pray for the sick.

On a trip to a youth conference in Ukraine, I had a ministry team wanting to go pray for healing. I told them, however, to wait. Instead of us doing all the praying, I wanted to get the Ukrainian students praying for the sick and see healings take place. My team trusted me, and later they understood why it was not yet time for us to pray for the sick. I wanted to first equip others so that they would be dependent on God and not on us.

- **One Word** - Everyone in the group has a pen and paper. Then everyone gives everyone in the group one word. At the end of the exercise, every person will have a list of words with which they can use to begin deciphering God's word to them using the three steps of revelation, interpretation, and application. This exercise helps participants relax and learn to prophesy from their spirit and not from their own thinking. The more one learns to tap into God's Spirit, the more one can tell when God's thoughts are your own.

What impedes people from prophesying, praying for healing, speaking in tongues, etc.? We think too much. We do not prophecy from our own thoughts, but from our spirit. This exercise enables people to relax and release one word, trusting God to speak through whatever we may say. At times, I have looked at a person and said a name of a relative or loved one. Other times it is simply a word such as "love" or "power." Do not judge a word by how deep or simple it may be.

Kris Valloton tells of a man telling a woman, "You have a yellow shirt on!"

The woman started weeping and crying hysterically. When asked why she reacted so, she explained, "I have a son who is autistic, and I told the Lord today, 'If You are going to heal my son, have someone tell me that I have on a yellow shirt….'"[47]

At another training, a woman looked at my shoes and told me, "God says 'Nike...Just do it.'"

What she did not know is that I always tell people to prophesy or heal the sick they need to: "Nike...Just do it." Her seemingly insignificant word was very significant for me.

You never know what a word may mean to someone. Don't try to figure everything out first. Just release it in faith and in a loving way.

- **The Blind Prophet** - The leader will pick out one individual who will then be blindfolded. This person will then be told to prophesy over someone in the group without them knowing who it is. It is fun when everyone in the group gets a number (even the person prophesying). Then the person blindfolded will prophesy over everyone including him/herself without knowing for whom they are prophesying.

This is the exercise where I often get the most significant words from people because they don't know they are prophesying over me. At times, people call me and ask me to prophesy over a group of people I do not know. It is great because I cannot depend on anything but the Holy Spirit to prophesy. I trust Him to speak through me. This exercise requires and develops strong faith to prophesy.

- **All on One** – One person stands in the middle of the group, and everyone in the group prophesies one by one over that person. This can be as simple as having one person sit in a chair in the middle of the room and everyone else share what they feel God may be saying.

  This is a great exercise to build up one person. I have seen the person in the middle extremely impacted by the prophetic words released over their lives during this exercise. Many people are not used to being strengthened, encouraged, and comforted by others. Expressing God's love is powerful. This is a great exercise to do before the following one.

- **One on All** – One person stands in the middle of the group and will prophesy over everyone in the group. This person's faith will be built up as they realize that they can prophesy over many people by faith.

  This exercise gets a person outside of their comfort zone. They do not have time to think, but must prophesy over the next person totally by faith. Whatever picture, Scripture, or feeling comes up, they must communicate that in a way that is strengthening, encouraging, and comforting.

- **Get Feedback** - Regularly stop between exercises and tell each other what the prophetic words have meant to one another. This is important to be able to test your prophetic flow and see where you are accurate and where you may be less accurate.

Getting feedback is very important in developing a prophetic ministry that remains accountable and transparent.

One man told a person he saw Switzerland and described things he saw. The person nodded and then told us how significant Switzerland was in his personal life. All the pictures and ideas he described had to do with a time of processing the loss of his wife, with whom he had spent much time with in Switzerland. Often we will say things and not have a clue what they mean to the person we are speaking to.

- **Sing a Prophecy** – Person(s) with a musical gift can take an instrument and start singing a prophecy. This can lead to new songs being written and often great authority is released with prophetic music.

  King David was a prophetic psalmist. Many worship leaders with a strong prophetic gifting should release songs prophetically. My brother has seen in his own ministry that at times when he begins prophesying through song, powerful manifestations of God's presence and even people oppressed by demons begin manifesting. Prophetic worship is powerful.

- **Prophesy Scripture** - Begin with a Scripture passage such as Psalm 23 and have team members read a Scripture and use that to begin prophesying over the person next to them. Random Scripture cards can also be used to help people get started. The goal, however, is that participants will be able to prophesy using Scripture that is in their own heart. Participants do not need to know where a Scripture is found. Just quote it and speak it forth as if it is God speaking those very words to their hearers.

  The Holy Bible is the inspired Word of God, and we can have a higher level of confidence when interpreting and applying

Scripture to people's lives. I am amazed how often God speaks through Scripture.

One Sunday I visited a church, and after service walked up to a man and said, "The just shall live by faith." I walked away not knowing that he was meditating on that Scripture all week long. He later told me how for an entire week the Lord had been speaking to him through the Scripture, "*The just shall live by faith*" (Hebrews 10:38).

- **Get the Picture** – By faith, ask God for a picture. This is as simple as a picture we see with our mind's eye (the eye of our imagination). When you see a picture, describe it and then by faith begin to share what you believe God could be saying through that picture. Follow the prophetic guidelines as you deliver this word.

  A picture is worth a thousand words and that is why God loves to speak through pictures. The dreams, pictures, and visions He has given remain with me for a long time. You never know when a picture is symbolic or a word of knowledge. While prophesying over a group of students, I told a woman that she was like a nurse and that I saw here taking care of babies. I then found out that she was studying to be a midwife. Tell what you see and say what you think it means. Then find out what it does mean to your hearer.

- **Random Object** - Have people in the group pick out a random object in the group and use that to deliver a word from God to someone in the room. The leader of the group can also call out a random object whereby participants may prophesy. This exercise is excellent to help people relax and know what to do when they feel they are stuck. If they are stuck, they can by faith grab a random object that serves as a diving board to start prophesying.

The editor of this book did not understand this activation, so I told him to name a random object in the room. He said, "The dog's bed." I then started prophesying that God was calling him to rest in His presence as a dog rests in his bed. He then responded that the previous night three people had prayed for him and all said God wanted him to rest.

- **Prophesy Over Someone Not Present** [48] - Have someone stand in the middle and think of someone they know, but don't have them reveal who it is. Participants can ask the person yes or no questions about the person. Once they begin realizing they are getting information about the person, have everyone prophesy over that person and have someone record the prophetic words for that individual. The person themself can decide whether it is appropriate to give the prophetic words given to that individual.

  There are many benefits of doing this exercise. Years ago I realized God would start speaking to me about people's children or family members who were not present. For example, I would think of the number two and ask a person how many children they had. If they had children, the word was possibly for their second child.

  Another benefit is that people can start learning how they may get words of knowledge. Shawn Bolz says that it may take time and practice before people get into the flow of getting accurate words of knowledge. He recalls how when living in Kansas City he would travel with friends and try to get words of knowledge for other people and not get anything right. However, God honored his hunger, and he eventually started getting accurate information about people. [49] God likes to reveal His secrets to his friends (see Amos 3:7).

- **Use a Diving Board** – Person in the middle asks God for information over the person(s) that is in front of him then use a "diving board" statement such as: *People have told you....... You have said....... Do you have pain in ....? Is there someone here who.........? When you were ... years old ....* After the "diving board" statement, let a word of knowledge flow. All information can be tested then to see if the person has tapped into the prophetic flow of revelation or if they are simply guessing.

One evening I visited a friend who gets up every morning at 4:30 am to pray. She spends significant time with God daily. I called some friends of mine and started giving her diving boards. "Tell them what happened yesterday," or, "Tell them what they have said or what other people have said about them." Ninety percent of what she said to people was accurate. She had a strong prophetic gift, but needed some help in activating and using the gift.

- **Write a Prophetic Message** – Everybody in the group gets a sheet of paper with a number on it. Without knowing whose number you have, write out a prophecy for that person. Feel free to begin with words such as, "*My dear child....*" or, "*Does not my word say...*" etc.

  This exercise activates the prophetic scribe. Being able to write a prophetic word is very useful.

- **Popcorn** – This exercise helps people learn to be able to prophesy quickly for those occasions when there may be one large group of individuals waiting to receive prophetic ministry. Learn to quickly give 30-60 second prophetic words to a line of 10-15 people. This exercise is great to force participants to prophesy from their spirit and do it by faith quickly. It also helps if 50 people are waiting for prophetic ministry and you only have a limited amount of time.

A prophetic word does not need to be long to be powerful and effective. At times, there is not much time to minister to everyone, so then do it quickly. I was praying before a large youth conference with the church leaders. I had less than five minutes to minister to over twenty people. I ministered to everyone with a ten to twenty second word. It was more than enough time to hear God speak to everyone in time to start the meeting.

- **Use a Motion** - Have a person stand up and use that motion as a diving board to prophesy how God is calling them to raise up in leadership, authority, etc. Other possible motions include: having them turn around, placing a crown on their head, lifting their hands, stomping on the ground, clapping their hands, washing feet, etc.

  The Bible is full of prophetic acts that prophets did to illustrate what God was going to do. Ezekiel dug a hole through the city wall (see Ezekiel 12:5). Hosea married Gomer, an unfaithful prostitute, whom he kept getting to come home (see Hosea). Jesus washed the feet of his disciples, and He blew on them to receive the Holy Spirit (see John 13:1-7 and 20:22). Motions and prophetic acts can be very powerful.

- **Wheel Inside of a Wheel** - Split the entire group into two different groups. Have one group make an interior circle and the rest of the other group surround them. The inner group will face the outer group and everyone in one group will prophesy over the other group. Have the people in the inside circle switch clockwise so that they will have a new person to prophesy over. After prophesying for a good while, have the outer group persons then prophesy over the inner group.

  This is a great exercise to get everyone prophesying and receiving prophetic words. Combine it with other exercises such as the blind prophet or using a diving board to change things up. I enjoy using this exercise at the end of prophetic evenings to be able to receive prophetic ministry and evaluate people's prophetic flow.

- **Ask God About Your Day** - At the beginning or end of your day, you can ask God what you might see or experience in the coming day. Write down what you see and or experience and see if it comes to pass. Some people like to ask God things about their waitress at a restaurant beforehand. They might right down on a napkin what they think or see. Then in casual conversation, they will ask about the details they wrote down. This is an easy way to test out immediately if what you are getting is accurate.

No matter which activations you may try, it is important to keep prophesying. I have many friends on social media, which means I can always send someone a prophetic message to them from time to time. Sometimes it may be simply a general encouraging word, and sometimes it can be an accurate word for a situation in their life. I don't worry about which one it is. I aim to strengthen, encourage, and comfort them. Don't worry about accuracy; be more concerned with loving Jesus and loving people the way He loves us. Your goal is not prophetic accuracy, but loving God and loving people.

Your goal is not prophetic accuracy, but loving God and loving people.

Chapter 7
Guidelines for Prophetic Ministry

"One who speaks a word of prophecy strengthens the entire church."
(1 Cor. 14:4b NLT)

"Therefore, my brothers and sisters, be eager to prophesy, and do not forbid speaking in tongues. But everything should be done in a fitting and orderly way."
(1 Cor. 14:39, 40)

Prophet Abel Brito did go through a time in his ministry when he used to call people out in front of a church and expose their sins. He recalls how he would tell everyone who was committing adultery and they would run down to the front and weep profusely saying it was true. He did this for a while until God told him, "Stop, I did not call you to expose people's sins. You are to be an extension of my mercy and my love."

Prophet's must be an extension of God's mercy. They are to be fountains of His love and mercy.[50]

A man walked up to me at a church once and said, "You are not going to tell everyone my sins, are you?"

I replied, "No. First of all, I don't know all of your sins. And secondly, that is not the primary goal of prophecy. Prophecy helps people see themselves the way that God sees them, so they can become what God wants them to be."

Prophetic ministry serves others and helps bring out the best in them.

Prophetic ministry serves others and helps bring out the best in them.

Bring Out the Best

Everyone looked down on little Zacchaeus as a traitor and a thief since he was the head of the tax collectors (Luke 19:1-10). Yet when Jesus saw him, he saw something very different. Jesus went to Zacchaeus' home and ate with him. This led to a radical change so that the "chief of sinners" became an extremely generous giver. Prophetic ministry changes lives because it enables people to see themselves as God sees them.

You've probably seen the mirrors in some amusement parks that warp your image. People love to see themselves get an oblong head or long body and little feet. But what may be amusing for a moment is tragic if people have a permanently warped self-image. When encountering Jesus, His words change our identity and our destinies. Prophetic ministry changes our image of God and of ourselves, and it is a tool God can use to correct our warped images.

After the repentant thief crucified next to Jesus spoke to Him, Jesus said that he would soon be in paradise with Him (see Luke 23:42). After an insane, demonized man encountered Jesus, he became an evangelist to an area of ten cities (see Luke 8:26-39). After Saul encountered Jesus, he changed from being a destroyer of the Church to one of its greatest champions (see Acts 9:1-19). God gives great honor to those who the world (and even other Christians) despises and sees as foolish (see 1 Cor. 1:27-28). Prophetic ministry is powerful because God can bring hidden gifts and talents to the surface that no one would have otherwise ever known about.

A prophet I know, recalls that in 1993, a prophet told him he was a prophet and someone free from reproach (guilt and shame). His reaction was, "That was very kind of her, but I am an electrician and not a prophet. Furthermore, I know I am full of reproach."

God was speaking to him about his *potential*, not his circumstances. God was speaking of who he would *become* and not the man he was at that moment. We prophesy into people's potential to encourage them with how God views them and not primarily about their sins and failures.

God can release a huge amount of authority and power when we prophesy. This can be used for good, but also for evil. This is why there must be guidelines and training available for those who want to grow in prophetic ministry. Good guidelines help avoid abuses.

Guidelines Help Avoid Abuses

A leader told me a story that illustrates abuse of prophetic ministry. The woman who had led him to the Lord and introduced him to the power of the Holy Spirit told him that God said he had to marry one of her relatives! He was a young new believer then and was confounded by this "word from God" that he had to marry someone he did not want to marry. "God, why are you forcing me to marry someone I don't want to marry?!" he prayed. Fortunately for both he and the young woman, he did not accept that misguided word.

Prophetic ministry is never to be used to manipulate others! Guidelines are present to help keep people safe and enable them to evaluate every prophetic word.

Jesus told His disciples that when the Holy Spirit would come upon them, they would receive power (see Acts 1:8). The word for power in Greek is *dunamis*, from which we get our word dynamite. Dynamite can be very useful to miners and construction workers or very dangerous if used by the unknowledgeable or, worse, evil people.

Disease, sicknesses, lies, and demonic strongholds can be destroyed through prophetic ministry, but if misused, people can also be destroyed. We must be mindful of how we handle prophecy and all the gifts of the Spirit. Just as anyone handling dynamite needs to follow safety guidelines, so we need to follow guidelines when prophesying.

Ten Guidelines for Developing Prophetic Ministry[51]

1. Always prophesy lovingly because love is the primary goal of all the gifts of the Holy Spirit (see 1 Cor. 12-14). Love God and love people. Do not prophesy if you are angry, bitter, or hurt. When you prophesy, you are reflecting the loving heart of God, and He is not angry, sad, or disappointed in people. Always prophesy into people's potential and not their problems. New Testament prophecy must always be for strengthening, encouragement, and, comfort (1 Cor. 14:3). Even when bringing a word of correction, do it in a way that brings hope and redemption.

Always prophesy into people's potential and not their problems.

2. Do not isolate yourself, but work together in teams. Our knowledge and our prophesying is not complete, and working together with teams is dynamic and healthy (see 1 Cor. 13:9). Learn to share the microphone with others and remain transparent and humble. Remember, the Biblical model is for prophets to train up other prophets in schools or companies of prophets (1 Samuel 19:18–24, 2 Kings 2, and 4:38-44). Do not compete with others; instead empower and encourage each other to grow in hearing God's voice. We don't *compete* with each other; we *complete* each other. We all prophesy in part, and when we all bring our part to the table then a bigger picture may be seen (see 1 Cor. 13:9).

3. Don't be too dramatic when you prophesy. Smile and be friendly when you prophesy. Feel free to say "perhaps" or "maybe" when you prophesy, but also recognize there may be moments when you can speak as if you are God, speaking in the first person (see 1 Peter 4:11). Don't let the message be lost because of the poor delivery. Communicate to others as God communicates with you—in a way they can understand.

4. Be sensitive for God and to people. Ask permission before you place your hand on someone. Place it on them softly and in an appropriate place. Be extremely sensitive regarding weddings, births, healings, and deaths. Be culturally sensitive when ministering in a different culture than your own. If you make a mistake, have the courage, humility, and integrity to apologize.

5. Never allow people to worship you. The goal of prophecy is to make Jesus great and not yourself (see John 3:30). We only reflect the light of God. Do not let encouraging comments inflate your ego. Instead genuinely redirect the praise to God. Beware of false humility.

6. NEVER give a prophetic word that is contrary to the Bible. Prophets must be students of the Bible who make the spiritual disciplines such as fasting, prayer, confession of sin, giving, etc., priorities in their lives. Every prophetic word that goes against Scripture is *wrong*. If something you say unknowingly goes against Scripture or is inaccurate, accept correction and see it as a chance to grow. The Holy Bible remains the source of our doctrine and not prophetic words.

7. Learn to give a prophetic word at the right moment and the right time. A prophet has control of himself/herself (see 1 Cor. 14:32). If it is not the right moment, hold onto it for the right time. You can also keep God's secrets. Learn to give a word from God at the right time and at the right moment. Also learn when not too prophesy too long. Don't be a microphone hog. Stop when God stops.

8. Every prophetic word must be tested. Welcome feedback. When you minister in a church, you submit to the authority of the local church. Prophets are servant-leaders who help build the church up. Cultivate genuine humility, and accept godly correction with a teachable spirit. Do not make a life changing

decisions based only on one prophetic word. If it is God speaking, He will confirm it to you as you seek Him.

9. Record every prophetic word possible. This enables the receiver to listen to the word and write it out. It enables other leaders to be able to test the word as well. It protects both parties from someone saying that something was said that was not said. Another person can take notes, but you can also use audio recordings.

10. Prophesy from *faith* and not only from feelings, sensations, or emotions (see Rom. 12:6) Learn to take risks and step out of your comfort zone while at the same time balancing that with the knowledge of what God has graced you to do and not to do. Always Remember 1 Corinthians 14:3— strengthen, encourage, and comfort.

People ministering prophetically embrace the guidelines of God's Word and common sense. We are free to operate within these guidelines that keep everyone involved safe. We must all be aware that we are human, and we will face human temptations such as using the influence of a prophetic voice to attempt to manipulate others for our own ends. We never use the credibility of a prophetic ministry for our own benefit, such as for personal or ministerial gain. We never attempt to manipulate or put a veneer of spirituality on our own inclinations or desires, such as "prophesying" people from other churches into our own ministry or telling people they must give us money by misusing God's name.

Any misuse of prophecy or its influence is unethical and totally inappropriate, and all prophets, teachers, and other ministers will have to account for their actions and statements to God. While we each must learn from mistakes, intentionally misleading people has dire consequences (see Matthew 18:5-6, Mark 9:41-42).

Frequently ask God to search your heart and examine your ways (see Psalm 139:23-24). If you have manipulated this way or feel tempted to do so, *stop* and repent. Ask God for people you can come into relationship with who can help coach or mentor you in prophetic ministry. Remember, we all make mistakes—it is part of the learning process. However, with a prophetic ministry also comes great responsibility. When we speak for God, we must always do so with pure, godly intentions.

Develop An Intimate Relationship with God

Many would like to grow in authority to prophesy, heal the sick, cast out demons, and move in the power of God. But authority comes primarily from our intimate relationship with God. As Dutch author Jan Pool short book series describes: "*Intimacy* with God allows us to anchor our *identity* in Christ so that we can then walk in His *authority.*"[52] An intimate relationship with God enables us to speak His words and do His works.

> An intimate relationship with God enables us to speak His words and do His works.

Our identity should stem from our secret, intimate relationship with God and not on how many people get healed or how accurate we may prophesy. An interesting example of this is the false prophets who were prophesying during the Jeremiah's time. Listen to what God says about them:

"But which of them has stood in the council of the Lord to see or to hear his words? Who has listened and heard his words?...<u>if they had stood in his council, they would have proclaimed my words</u> to my people and would have turned them from their evil ways and from their evil deeds" (Jeremiah 23:22 emphasis added).

Those false prophets could have been true prophets if they would have learned to stand in the presence of God and listen and watch what He had to say. If we want to be true prophets, or spokespeople for God, we need to prioritize our intimate time with God. We must routinely and periodically go before His throne (see Hebrews 4:16).

Spiritual disciplines (prayer, fasting, Bible Study, etc.) are a way of life for all mature prophets who I know. No one becomes a prophet in one day. Everyone must go through a process of growth in which they will inevitably have successes and failures. These guidelines enable us to grow in the times that we have successes in ministry, but also when we make mistakes. Here are some of my own successes and blunders in prophetic ministry.

Successes In Prophetic Ministry

In 2015 in Czech Republic, I walked up to a lifeguard at a swimming pool and told him that God wanted him to write a book. What I did not know was that he had just written a book that had accidentally been deleted from his hard drive. He had told God that if it was His will for him to rewrite the book, then someone had to tell him that God wanted him to write a book. That was the beginning of a great friendship and open doors to serve in many churches in Czech Republic.

In March 2010, a prophet in Chicago told me God was opening up the Spirit for me and I was going to try to preach a prepared sermon. He said God would have me preach something totally different. Three weeks later, it happened.

I was at a large church in Oklahoma when I noticed that I had to preach something totally different than what I had planned. I also started stepping out into the audience and prophesying over individuals. I ended the meeting by lining up ten men and prophesying over every one of them. After the sermon, the pastor sat me down and said, “Everything you were prophesying was accurate. Son, from an old preacher to a young preacher, forget your sermon and follow the Spirit."

I was excited to say the least, but the day was not over. That evening, I prophesied over an entire church group, and afterwards the server at a Subway restaurant was shocked when I gave him an accurate word of knowledge. The evening ended with me being able to pray for him. To say that I was excited, would be an understatement.

Blunders in Prophetic Ministry

The next morning, I got out of bed early wanting to prophesy over another stranger. I walked through the neighborhood looking for someone I could talk to. I saw a man's door open and went to give him a "word from God."

Ten minutes later, a police officer came after me! "Throw that stick down on the ground!" (I was walking with a stick in my hand.) "Are you on drugs? Why are you shaking?" the police officer said to me.

"I am shaking because you are a police officer," was my reply.

After the officer identified me and got my address, she told me that someone called because they saw me talking to myself and I gave them a message from God. When I went home, I bawled like a baby. "Dad, I really messed up. I brought shame to the name of God. I really, really messed up and I am so sorry."

That person thought I was crazy, dangerous, and I seriously learned a valuable lesson. How I give a message to someone is just as or even *more* important than the word itself.

The Bible says that the word of God is like a double-edged sword able to do heart surgery between people's soul and spirit (see Hebrews 4:12). The way we use the Bible and the gift of prophecy can either be like a butcher or like a medical surgeon. Both of those metaphors are scary, yet I never want to be mistaken as a butcher when using the gift of prophecy.

As anyone suffering with cancer welcomes the knife of a surgeon to remove a cancerous tumor, so I hope that we will allow God to use His words to cut things out of our lives so that we can become healthy. Similarly, I want His words through me to be like a surgeon who can help bring healing and new life by cutting out the lies of the enemy from someone's heart.

After spending Saturday evening at an African church in South East Amsterdam, I preached Africa-style (very loudly) at a "white" Dutch church. Apparently, my African style preaching scared people, and I may never speak at that church again. I learned I must be sensitive to where I am—to context. What may be the correct way to speak in one place may be the wrong way to speak at another. The way you prophesy is just as important as what you prophesy. This is why I always try to prophesy with a calm and happy face now.

The way you prophesy is just as important as what you prophesy.

Always ask people for permission to pray for them and ask if you can share what you feel God saying! Remember you are just the deliveryman (or woman), and you cannot force someone to accept a message.

One waitress at a restaurant misinterpreted my saying that I wanted to share the love of God with people; instead of encouraging her, I scared her. When I told her something about her daughter, she really freaked out. At other times, I have seen people get healed and start saying, "This is scary!"

Always try to make supernatural ministry natural and not weird. When approaching people you don't know, relax and remain kind and friendly. The power of God works best when we are at peace. Your goal is not to impress people with a spiritual gift but to bring them closer to Jesus. Avoid acting like a used car salesman, but really care about people. Caring about people also means you do not have to say everything you know or feel.

Your goal is not to impress people with a spiritual gift, but to bring them closer to Jesus.

Using power and revelation gifts (prophecy, healing, words of knowledge, etc.) **NEVER** gives us permission to be rude, arrogant, or obnoxious. Jesus was humble and gentle in spirit, and so we must reflect the heart of Jesus in the way we behave (see Matt. 11:29). Approach people in a way that they know you want to serve them and help them. Do not be offended when people reject your offer to pray for them.

One family received prophetic ministry simultaneously by a large group of people. The result was confusion. Instead of them being encouraged, they were left with their heads spinning in confusion from all the different shotgun prophetic words. The delivery of a word must be done in an orderly way so people can hear, understand, and begin to process what God may be saying.

I have also seen young prophets who are extremely accurate but who are still immature. Some people think being emotional and dramatic is a prerequisite of moving prophetically. It is not and can be counterproductive if ministering in a culture which does not trust emotionalism. Being weird or mystical is not necessary to give someone a word from God. However, it is necessary that we remain humble and teachable to continue growing in this ministry.

On more than one occasion, I have had to apologize because something I said or did was misunderstood. This can be messy and even painful, but being transparent, teachable, and humble are crucial for growing in maturity. The heart of a minister is more important than what great signs and wonders he or she may do. True prophetic ministry is not about getting a big ego, but about making Jesus great and loving people like God loves us.

The "Blunders" Build Character

Not everyone I pray for gets healed. Not every word of knowledge or prophetic word is always one hundred percent right. This is why Paul says to judge and test every prophetic word (see 1 Cor. 14:29 and 1 Thess. 5:19-22).

It forces me to remain humble as I endeavor to grow in prophetic ministry. I can rejoice when a word of knowledge is accurate and, when necessary, I can also apologize if it is not. Failures are also not really failures if we learn from them. We grow from them, and that adds to our successes.

As Kenneth Hagin once said, "If I am wrong, I want to get it right. If I miss it, I just admit, 'I missed it.' Don't be afraid to say, 'I missed it.' When I first started learning to drive a car, I missed it a few times and ran over the curb. But I didn't quit driving just because I missed it. Did you? We ought to have as much sense about spiritual things. Just because I missed it, I am not going to quit. I am going to keep going."[53]

I was teaching once about words of knowledge and the necessity of testing every word. I walked up to a young woman and told her about something that took place when she was thirteen years old. Then I asked her if it happened and she said, "As far as I can remember, no."

I felt horrible. I wanted to go dig a hole and hide, but then I realized how important it is to show that everyone can make a mistake, and it is imperative that every word be evaluated and tested. People learn the most not just when we show our strengths, but also our weaknesses.

I finished my teaching session and then gathered my team to talk and pray. I felt like a puppy licking his wounds, but my team reassured me of the importance of not just showing your strengths but illustrating that God can also use my weaknesses. When we share our weaknesses, we can show people that God can use them too.

I heard Randy Clark tell a story about healing meetings with John Wimber.[54] On a Friday night healing meeting, it seemed like one hundred percent of the people present were healed. Saturday night, no one got healed. Clark said that Wimber said something like, "I know, before you say anything, all I can do is stick out my fat hand and say, 'Come Holy Spirit.' Whether they get healed or not is not up to me."

This story was an inspiration for Randy Clark as well as all of us who endeavor to grow in the healing ministry.

Your *character* is even more important than how many people get healed or your accuracy in prophetic ministry. Are you generous, loving, kind, honest, submissive, and teachable? Are you someone who prays, fasts, and serves the people around you? Are you secure enough to listen to people who may disagree or strongly dislike you? Jesus made it clear that we are to rejoice and be glad when people insult us, persecute us, and say all kinds of evil against us (see Matthew 5:12). That is a skill that I have still not fully developed, but you will need it!

Your *character* is even more important than how many people get healed or your accuracy in prophetic ministry.

It is extremely important that prophetic people do not take on the spirit of those who antagonize them and return evil for evil, but instead strive to overcome evil with goodness and kindness (see Rom. 12:21). Character, spiritual disciplines, rest, accountability, humility, and holiness are vital. Prophets may be able to function temporarily without some of these, but sooner or later you will become ineffective, unproductive, self-destructive, or even worse.

I have heard it said that it is better to burn out than to rust out, but I opt for neither. I want to have many years of a long-term productive ministry. That requires developing and maintaining character and integrity and always following principles and guidelines that makes prophetic ministry a blessing and never a curse.

Proverbs 14:4 says where the manger is full, the ox works hard and brings in a great harvest. However, the manger may be messy if an ox is regularly feeding there. Prophetic and healing ministry can also be messy. This is why prophetic protocol needs to be established and followed for the safety of everyone involved.

A pastor once told me about a psychological test that was done with two groups of mice. The first group of mice would press certain buttons and would be rewarded with delicious food. These mice would press the buttons as often as possible to get some more delicious food. They were delighted and always wanted to push the buttons for some more.

The second group of mice received an electric shock instead of food when they pushed a button. This second group of mice refused to ever touch a button again for the rest of their lives because of this unpleasant experience. Those who have experienced unpleasant things regarding prophecy or spiritual gifts will not be open to learning more about it. Guidelines enable us to guard the prophetic ministry so that people do not unnecessarily get burned.

One pastor told me that years earlier, he had a strong and healthy group of prophetic ministers in his church. However, at one point, a new person came in to lead that ministry and effectively destroyed it. That individual refused to submit or work together with the pastor and the other church leaders. She thought she heard God's voice and nobody else did. Her refusal to abide by a prophetic protocol damaged the church and the prophetic ministry.

This leader had nearly given up on prophetic ministry until we came with a prophetic team to serve his church. We loved, honored, and served him and his people. After that conference, several churches in his city began regularly prophesying and healing the sick in church services as well as on the streets. He thanked us for modeling healthy prophetic ministry that seeks to always build the church up and never tear it down. We must abide by prophetic guidelines if we want to see a prophetic ministry develop that is effective for the long haul.

Chapter 8
How to Grow in Words of Knowledge

"A word of knowledge is a supernatural revelation about a fact about a person or a situation that does not come from human thoughts, but from the Spirit of God. It is one of the revelatory gifts which include words of knowledge, wisdom, prophecy and discernment." -David Betts, Amsterdam 2010 New Wine Conference

"Getting a word of knowledge is often very subtle; more often than not, we think that it is us instead of God. Stepping out in risk is the only way we will find out if we are hearing God correctly."- Putty Putman, School of Kingdom Ministry

"But if all of you are prophesying, and unbelievers or people who don't understand these things come into your meeting, they will be convicted of sin and judged by what you say. As they listen, their secret thoughts will be exposed, and they will fall to their knees and worship God, declaring, 'God is truly here among you.'" (1 Cor. 14:24-25, NLT)

When I was preaching in a church in Budapest, I turned around and told a man, "God is going to use you to bring a lot of resources of finances and help to this church."

My interpreter said, "That is a word of knowledge. He is already doing that."

"Great! Well, tell him that God is going to continue using him this way," I responded.

Sometimes people ask me what the difference is between a word of knowledge and a prophetic word. To be honest, when I am prophesying, I do not necessarily know when a word I am giving is a word of knowledge, a word of wisdom, a discernment of spirits, or when I may shift into healing ministry. All the gifts of the Holy Spirit work together. They are like the Olympic rings on the Olympic flag that are all interwoven with one another. When you activate the prophetic gift, the other gifts of the Holy Spirit may become active as well.

During a dinner, I began prophesying over a friend. Suddenly I saw a mental picture of a backbone and found out he had pain in his back. I prayed for him, and he felt heat going through his back as all the pain left. I did not plan on praying for his back, but as I began prophesying, I got a word of knowledge and then shifted into praying for healing. God is extremely generous, and the more gifts we give away, the more gifts He can continue giving us.

God is extremely generous, and the more gifts we give away, the more gifts He can continue giving us.

My brother Aaron is regularly aware of demonic oppression in the lives of people or even churches. Through the operation of the discernment of spirits, he has seen many people and churches set free from that oppression. He does not know when God will use each gift when he ministers, but whatever God reveals to him, he uses to bring healing and deliverance to people's lives.

At psychic fairs, I minister to everyone who comes to our table using the gifts of the Holy Spirit, and I have seen Jesus heal and speak to many people at such places. I never know when a word I give to someone may be simply a general encouraging word or a very detailed description of their lives.

At one psychic fair near Amsterdam, two people sat down at my table. I proceeded to tell one of them about their work and the things that had happened in the recent past and the things that needed to be done in the next six months. I described her role and responsibility.

The words of knowledge kept flowing, and I was amazed at the level of details and information I was giving her.

Twenty minutes later, she told me everything I said was true and she was amazed. I was so excited that I got to use words of knowledge to show that Jesus is real and that He cares for her and her work. Words of knowledge show people that God is real and help them increase their faith for God to touch them.

One man who came to a meeting I was prophesying at was shocked when I asked him what his wife's name was and proceeded to say, "She loves you very, very much!"

What I did not know is that he had just had an argument with his wife and had left the house saying, "Do you still love me?!" God let him know that his wife loved him very much even though they had just had an argument.

I regularly use words of knowledge when I do "power evangelism." Instead of beginning a conversation talking about Jesus, I ask people if I can tell them what I see in them. If they say yes, I ask God for a word of knowledge and go for it. Sometimes I may say something that is not completely right, but often people do say, "How did you know that?"

This becomes an open door to talk to people about Jesus who otherwise would not be interested in talking about Him at all. A word of knowledge or a healing is a fantastic doorway to show that Jesus is real.

Some examples of Jesus using words of knowledge are His instructions to His disciples and His conversations with Nathaniel, Peter and the woman at the well. Let's take a look at how Jesus used words of knowledge.

Jesus' Instructions to the Disciples[55]

"Go into the village over there," he said. "As soon as you enter it, you will see a donkey tied there, with its colt beside it. Untie them and bring them to me. If anyone asks what you are doing, just say, 'The Lord needs them,' and he will immediately let you take them" (Matthew 21:2-3).

Jesus gave instructions to His disciples where to go and who to talk to, to get things done. He told Peter once to go fishing and pull a coin out of the first fish he would catch (see Matthew 17:27). Through words of knowledge, Jesus can still tell us where to go and who to talk to, to share His love and power.[56]

I took a group of Bible school students to a shopping center in Amersfoort, the Netherlands. As we drove there, we asked God for words of knowledge. Three words popped up: a bread bakery, Mary, and back pain.

After ten minutes of walking around, two excited students came to me saying, "We went to the bread bakery and Mary was standing outside and she had back pain. We prayed for her, and the pain disappeared."

Using accurate words of knowledge to share the love and power of Jesus to people is valuable and fun.

Jesus' Conversation with Nathanael

When Philip told Nathanael about going to visit Jesus, his reaction was cynicism and unbelief. *"Can anything good come out of Nazareth?"* (John 1:46).

The words of knowledge which caused Nathanael to believe were a description of him being a person of honesty and integrity and he had sat under a fig tree the day before when Philip called him (see John

1:47-48). Such a simple word about a fig tree changed Nathanael from being cynical and unbelieving to totally being open.

At one prophetic evening, a man told me he was unhappy because all the words given to him were general and vague. He wanted us to tell him something no one knew.

I hate being pushed in a corner, but one of my friends said, "Yeah, let us do it."

We started praying for him, and I told him about some things that took place in his childhood. When we were done, he said, "Ok, you guys both said things you could never know."

Though this may not always work this way, I was thankful for God giving us some information about his life at that moment that showed him God really cared.

During a prophetic evening near Utrecht, the Netherlands, I gave a prophetic word to a woman. She understood perfectly the first half of what I said, but understood nothing about the second half. It was about a time of great warfare coming in her life, but that she would see Jesus at the end of the battle.

Four months later, the leader of that group told me that that woman was diagnosed six weeks after that meeting with an aggressive form of cancer and within a short period of time passed away. For her, the words, "You will see Jesus" brought her great comfort in that time of sickness and death. Little did I know what those words meant nor how much they would strengthen her in the last days of her life!

Jesus' Conversation with the Samaritan Woman at the Well

Jesus encountered a Samaritan woman at a well that led to an entire group of people from her village believing in Him. During this conversation, He revealed that she'd had five husbands and that she was now living in an adulterous relationship. However, He did not use this information to put her down. Instead, Jesus spoke into her potential of becoming a true worshipper. She ran back to her village believing in Christ and telling her friends, *"Come and see a man who told me everything I ever did! Could he possibly be the Messiah?"* (John 4:29).

Jesus spoke into her potential of becoming a true worshipper.

Words of knowledge can be life changing!

In 2014 and 2015, I was invited to train Bible school students in prophetic ministry so that they could be the prophetic ministry team at a large youth event in Pennsylvania. For two days, I had the privilege of being a wandering prophet going to different individuals and groups prophesying over them during worship and special moments set aside for prophetic ministry.

In 2015, I got to hear all of the testimonies from 2014. One pastor told me, "It was surreal. You walked into the room and walked up to me and told me everything that God has been telling me in the last six months. Then you walked back and added some other things that He has been challenging us about. It was amazing."

When we cultivate an atmosphere of worship and a culture where the supernatural can naturally take place, amazing things can take place. My greatest joy, however, is not in how God may use *me* but how he uses those who I get to train.

One woman who was a new believer, stood up on the platform giving words of knowledge that led to people getting healed. When young people experience the legitimate power of God, it is fun and life-changing.

How You May Get A Word of Knowledge[57]

There are many ways to get a word of knowledge. Four possible ways are: seeing it, hearing it, speaking it and feeling it. Let's look at each of them.

Seeing A Word of Knowledge

In 2009, I was at a prayer meeting in London when a woman walked up to me and said, "I see the word discouragement on your head, but that God has wiped that away." Her words were accurate. I had just gone through a time of discouragement, but I was entering a new time where I was very encouraged.

God can show us pictures that may be literal or symbolic, which means that many times we will have to interpret them. However, we will not know if they are literal or symbolic unless we share them. These pictures or words are things we see in our "mind's eye" and can be superimposed upon people or things. We may also see or experience the presence of God, angels, or demons at times. This is part of the gift of discernment of spirits.

My brother will often see a mental picture of different body parts that God is about to heal during worship. Once he starts ministering, he describes what he saw, and many people are healed through those words of knowledge.

My mother once saw a vision while praying that the landlord where my parents lived would ask them to move out of their house. The next week, everything that she saw in the vision literally took place just as she had seen it. God can give us information through daytime visions and nighttime dreams.

Feeling a Word of Knowledge

If you start getting a pain or emotion that does not belong to you, that might be a word of knowledge. I was in Eastern Europe once when a woman on my team told me, "I am getting really afraid suddenly. In fact, I am literally shaking with fear."

I told her, "Relax. It is a word of knowledge. You are picking up a strong spirit of fear in this region."

A prophet on my ministry team was at one of our meetings when she started struggling with thoughts of doubts and cynicism. She thought, "This prophecy stuff is all false. None of this is real."

She recognized that these were not her thoughts. She looked next to her, and there were about six people with their arms crossed refusing to do any of the activations. She went ahead and started prophesying over them, and they started opening up. She realized she was picking up their thoughts and they were not her own.

About the ministry of healing, if you are suddenly feeling pain somewhere, it could be a word of knowledge that God wants to heal someone of that condition. Feel free to ask, "Does someone have pain here?" If someone does, pray—and do not be surprised when they get healed!

Hearing a Word of Knowledge

One Sunday I woke up with a name in my mind. Nobody at the church I visited that Sunday had that name. Later that week, I was in England and prophesied over a pastor—that God would use him mightily in Italy. I then found out that he had just been in Italy and he had been ministering to a pastor who lived in a city with the same name that I had woken up thinking about earlier that week.

I have never heard the audible voice of God with my physical ears, but I have heard Him speak loudly in my heart. There are times when He has given me names of places to which I would travel and minister. Normally, I just keep that information to myself and see when, how, and if it would come to pass.

You may also hear a play on words or a riddle. One day, I heard the name "DES-I-DER-IUS" and "DE-SID-UOUS." I looked it up and stumbled upon the famous Dutch reformer Desiderius Erasmus. I felt like God was speaking to me about his desire to use me as a Dutch leader who will help bring change.

The "deciduous" word led me to the deciduous trees, which are always green year around. I started praying Psalm 1:3 about being like a tree planted by streams of water that always bears fruit in season.

Also, before deciding to get involved in ministry to prostitutes, I was praying when suddenly I heard the words loudly in my spirit say, "SET MY PEOPLE FREE!" I felt like God was speaking and confirming His desire that we help people find true freedom.

Speaking a Word of Knowledge

My mother once received a cake from our neighbors in Chile. As she started to cut it, suddenly the words came out of her mouth, "There is glass inside of the cake."

Sure enough, she cut open the cake and found pieces of glass inside of it. The neighbors had broken a bottle of milk accidentally and pieces of the glass had fallen inside of the cake batter. That "automatic mouth" where something just popped out of her mouth may have saved someone's life.

This is also part of developing a prophetic flow. Sometimes while prophesying I will say things such as, "There are three things that are important in your life right now."

Then I pray, "God what are those three things?"

As I speak, those three things I did not know come out of my mouth.

How to Deliver a Word of Knowledge[58]

Words of knowledge can be simply a quick flash of a thought or feeling that can easily be explained away as something you yourself are making up. Anyone can get a word of knowledge, and that is why it is important that people learn to be aware that what they may be experiencing "could" be a word of knowledge.

Offer words of knowledge to people, and do not impose them on them. For example, I heard someone say that they walked up to a pregnant woman and said, "It is going to be a boy, and you have to name him Jeremiah."

That person went over the woman's boundaries. No one can force someone else to do something they don't want to through a word of knowledge. That person could have offered her a suggestion, "Hey, if it is a boy, consider the name Jeremiah."

Remember, how you deliver a word is just as important as the word itself.

Know that you may be wrong, but don't worry about it if you are! Deliver it in a way that is gracious and humble. Many times, I will give a word of knowledge and no one will respond until after the service or days later saying that they were the person I was describing.

At times, you may use a springboard such as: People have said to you that ________. You have said ________ or when you were ____ years old______. This is a step of faith where you simply say whatever comes out of your mouth after you have started the springboard.

Please get feedback. If you were right, then you know it was the Holy Spirit. If you are wrong, know that you may have missed it. Learning from mistakes will help your become a better prophetic minister.

During a School of Prophecy in Amsterdam, a leader from my church was prophesying over different individuals, encouraging, strengthening, and comforting people. I was aware, though, that if she would take some risks, she could get more revelation about the past, the present, and the future of individuals. I told her then, "Go ahead and tell people what they have said, what has taken place, or what may take place in their lives."

She went for it and looked at me and said, "I see you on the airplane from Ukraine and there is a woman with red pants and grey hair sitting next to you."

Afterwards she looked at me and said, "Will you please let me know if it really happens?"

As I was flying back from the Ukraine, I looked across the aisle from me and there was the woman with red pants and grey hair. That word of knowledge was spot on.

Words of Knowledge From An Entire Group

In Acts 13, the church of Antioch was full of prophets and teachers who asked God for knowledge of what He wanted them to do next. They prayed and fasted, and the Holy Spirit spoke clearly to them. We read,

> *While they were worshiping the Lord and fasting, the Holy Spirit said, 'Set apart for me Barnabas and Saul for the work to which I have called them.' So after they had fasted and prayed, they placed their hands on them and sent them off* (Acts 13:2-3).

In 1967, my father was a student at Oral Roberts University. The school had chosen to take three students to Chile for special meetings, and my father tells of how the decision was made who was to go of all the students.

> Reuben Sequeira, a classmate of mine, was passing through the hall of the Timko-Barton Building, when he happened upon the seminary professors talking in the hall. They were discussing on how to select students from the seminary to go on this initial preparatory trip to Chile. Their discussion went something like this:
>
> "How in the world are we going to pick just three of the seminary students to go to Chile? We would like to send all sixty of them!"
>
> Reuben could not hold back from speaking up when he heard that. He said:
>
> "You are all Spirit-filled men of God. You all have your doctorates in theology, don't you? Why don't you just ask God who He wants to send?"
>
> His words hit home! They went into an empty classroom nearby, knelt, and asked God to reveal to them which three seminary students were to go as student representatives of the seminary. Then they each wrote down three names that came to them. When they compared the names, they were all the same! God had answered their prayer!
>
> The three names each one wrote down individually were the three students who went! And that is how I was selected to go to Chile in April of 1967, never suspecting that I would eventually spend fifteen years of my life there with my family, working with the national Pentecostal churches!"[59]

The prayers of those professors led to a decision that would change my father's life, and my life as well. We can expect God to speak to us because it is His pleasure to reveal things to us (see Ephesians 1:9). We grow in words of knowledge and gifts of the Spirit by humbly and courageously asking God for them. We must endeavor to grow in them

Endeavor to Grow in Using Words of Knowledge

When going to do evangelism on the street, I ask God for information ahead of time. Sometimes nothing I write down takes place and other times it does.

When taking a team in Fresno to the streets, we realized about 50% of the things we had written down took place. We did not mourn what did not happen, we celebrated what did. Part of growing in words of knowledge is taking risks, which may or may not be rewarded immediately or at all.

In November of 2016, I gave several words of knowledge in a church in Kiev to which no one responded. I asked if there was anyone who had a car accident in 2013 and was suffering from back pain. No one responded in a church with over a thousand people present.

In May of 2017, I was back in Kiev teaching on words of knowledge at a youth camp. A member of my ministry team saw random numbers and he did not know what they meant. The numbers corresponded to the license plate of a man who had a car accident in 2013. His back had been healed earlier that morning during the session on divine healing.

Don't worry about a time lag between when you give a word of knowledge and whether someone responds to it. There was a six-month time lag between when I gave that word of knowledge and when I met the man who had the car accident in 2013.

I was speaking at a youth group once when I got a pain in my wrist, which was a word of knowledge. A woman came forward with pain in her wrist and was healed after I prayed for her. Then I got pain right in the middle of my back between my shoulder blades. I asked if anyone had pain there and nobody responded.

What I did not know was that the same woman whose wrist was healed had a sister-in-law with pain in that exact same spot. However, she did not dare come forward to ask prayer for her sister-in-law who was not present. The next day she told her sister-in-law about the word of knowledge, and at that moment, she was healed!

They thought I must have prayed for her or done something special. In reality all I said was, "Does anyone have pain right here in your back?"

That word of knowledge released faith for her to be healed. Accurate words of knowledge release faith in people's hearts and show them that God is real and that He loves them. They can challenge people to do things they never thought of doing.

In the spring of 1909, pastor and former missionary A.G. Garr received the name J.H. King from God while praying. He then contacted King, who was then the general overseer of Fire-Baptized Holiness Church. He told him that God wanted him to travel the world and preach the Gospel. King disagreed with this "word from God" and returned home to all his responsibilities. But this word would not let him go.

On September 20, 1910 J. H. King left on a two-year preaching tour of the world. During his absence, his church merged with the Holiness Church of North Carolina and became known as the International Pentecostal Holiness Church. A word of knowledge played an important role in launching him and the church he led into international ministry.[60] Words of knowledge can lead us to do things we would have never considered. I am honored to be a part of this church and carry on the work of preaching the Gospel around the world using prophecy, words of knowledge, and healing.

Chapter 9
Creating the Future

"Only I can tell you the future before it even happens..."
Isaiah 46:10 (NLT)

"But when he, the Spirit of truth, comes, he will guide you into all the truth. He will not speak on his own; he will speak only what he hears, and he will tell you what is yet to come." ***John 16:13***

In 2013, I was preaching at a Hispanic church in Oklahoma City when the following words popped out of my mouth, "Two years from now, you will no longer be in this building, but in another larger building." I was shocked when those words came out of my mouth so then I added (just in case), "And two years from now, we will find out if that was really God speaking or just me."

Two years later, the church moved into a much larger building.

In March of 2016, I walked up to a man I did not know, in Broken Arrow, Oklahoma, and told him I felt God was going to give him his own business. He thought, "There is no way that is going to happen."

In October, he told me it really happened. His boss unexpectedly decided to sell his business to him.

I am elated when this happens, and I am more than willing to share the secret of how to foretell the future. It has nothing at all to do with knowing the future, but it has everything to do with knowing the one who knows the future: God.

In Psalm 105:15, 18, 19 we can see how this principle worked in the life of Joseph. *"Do not touch my anointed ones; do my prophets no harm... He sent a man before them—Joseph, sold as a slave. They bruised his feet with shackles, his neck was put in irons, till* ***what he foretold*** *came to pass, till* ***the word of the Lord*** *proved him true*" (emphasis added).

Joseph could foretell the future because he simply said what he heard God say.

Joseph could foretell the future because he simply said what he heard God say.

Jesus said that He could do nothing Himself. He only said what He heard the Father saying and did what He heard the Father doing (see John 5:19; 12:49-50).

Prophets often know very little about a person or situation and much of what they may know is only a part of the whole picture (see 1 Cor. 13:9). They only know what God reveals to them. However, God says that He does nothing without revealing His plans or His secrets to His servants the prophets (see Amos 3:7). God loves to reveal His secrets to His friends, and many times He does that by whispering His secrets to them when they learn to be quiet (see 1 Kings 19:12).

One of the most important Scriptures that I am still trying to apply to my life is Psalm 46:10, which says, *"Be still and know that I am God."*

God, Please Sell That House!

I remember one day I was facing a problem because, due to the economic crisis in the Netherlands, my old house was not selling and I was facing the prospect of having to pay two mortgages. I remember praying repeatedly, "God, tell me what to do."

"Trust me," was his response.

"No, really, God, you need to tell me what to do. Just tell me what to do now," I responded repeatedly.

"Trust me," was all He kept repeating back to me. I decided to trust Him.

During this crisis, I called a friend and asked him to pray for me. As he did, he said, "God says the second buyer will buy your house."

I was not happy. I didn't want a second buyer. I wanted *one* buyer and that house to sell ASAP!

The day that we moved into our new house, the first buyers backed out of the deal and informed us that they did not want to buy the house anymore.

I went into crisis mode. I went and spent two hours in my (new) attic, prayerfully and tearfully yelling at God, "GOD, PLEASE SELL THAT HOUSE!"

Four days later, at 10:00 in the morning, the old house was sold to the second buyer.

This entire experience was a huge lesson for me that caused my prayer life to increase significantly. I realized that it had taken a crisis for me to spend significant time in prayer because I needed something from God. At that point, I decided that I was going to spend at least one hour a day simply praying. Through this crisis, I got to know God better. It is unfortunate that sometimes it may take a crisis for us to seek God.

Another way that God enables us to know the future is simply by giving us the desires in our heart.

Hello, Welcome To Git-n-Go.

Hundreds of times a day, I would repeat this phrase to the customers who would come into the gas station I worked at for two summers as a teenager. I remember that during the second summer I had a burning desire inside of me to become a Bible teacher at a kid's summer camp. While I dreamed of teaching children the Bible, I would proceed to restock the pop, cigarettes, and beer, and once again greet the incoming customers with, "Hello, welcome to Git-n-Go."

Nine months later, I met the director of a kids' summer camp located fifteen minutes from my house who hired me to become the Bible teacher. That summer, over three hundred children prayed to accept Christ at the little chapel in the woods! This experience taught me some important lessons about how God can show us the future.

I had a desire to teach the Bible to kids, but it was not time yet. This meant that I needed to simply be faithful at the gas station, working hard and serving people. Because I was faithful in the little, then God could put me over much more (see Luke 16:10).

Sometimes I encounter individuals who want God to use them mightily, however they are not faithful in the little unglamorous things no one sees. A local church is a great place for God to develop our character. This could be as simple as taking care of children or helping set up chairs. Even though this may not seem exciting or glamorous, our character is formed when nobody is looking. What you do when nobody is looking is more important than when everybody is looking.

> What you do when nobody is looking is more important than when everybody is looking.

In seventh grade, I started playing basketball without having a clue how to shoot a ball. On television, I saw Michael Jordan score every time he shot the ball, and thought I would do the same. My first game was very disappointing. I did not score a single basket. My basketball career did not look very promising.

For the rest of the year, I spent time every day after school shooting baskets. I got some good coaching, and by the end of the eighth grade, I could shoot the ball and score (once in a while). The secret to my growth was in practicing when no one else was watching. It is the same in God's kingdom; if we are faithful in the secret place, then God can reward us publicly. It is our secret prayers, Bible study, fasting, and giving that enables us to bear fruit in our public lives.

God is more interested in *who we are* than in *what we do* for Him because what we do comes out of who we are. Our society drives us to be human *doings*, yet God has made us to be human *beings*.

Even the name of God is not "I do what I do," but *"I am that I am"* (Exodus 3:14). This is why learning to sit down and be still is so important to hear God's voice. Learning to simply "be" and not always have to "do" is important. Once we learn to connect to God in the secret place, we can learn to live connected continually to Him no matter where we are and what we are doing (see 1 Thess. 5:16-18).

Our character and skills are formed by what we do when nobody is watching us. This applies to sports, music, and to prophetic ministry. If God puts desires in our hearts, He will fulfill them on His time schedule.

Don't seek success; connect to God and His kingdom, and He will take care of the rest (see Matt. 6:33).

Don't seek success; connect to God and His kingdom, and He will take care of the rest.

You Will Go to New York City.

In July 2000, during a time of worship, I felt like God told me that I was to go to New York City and learn how to do "Sidewalk Sunday School." I did not tell anyone about this and asked God to confirm this if it was His will. Six months later, leaders from a ministry in NYC gave me a personal invitation to be a part of their internship program. I had a great peace about this decision as well as my parent's blessing. It would lead me to one of the most important decisions of my life: marrying Femke, which would eventually lead me to living in the Netherlands.

God will make His desire for our lives clear, and we can trust Him with every decision. When it comes to making important decisions, we can trust Him to reaffirm His will to us in many different ways. We can remain at peace regarding important decisions. We don't have to place pressure on ourselves to make God's plans happen on our time schedule. "*Trust in the Lord with all your heart. Lean not on your own understanding. In all your ways acknowledge Him and he will make your paths straight,"* is one hundred percent true (Proverbs 3:5-6).

Life is not about the destination, but about enjoying the journey along the way. God is able to do more than we ask or imagine in our lives, yet it begins in the little things we do. If we say yes to God in a lot of little things, then we can say yes in the big things as well. If we learn to hear God daily through Bible study and prayer, it will be easier to hear his voice concerning the big decision such as who you should marry.

Should I Marry Femke?

In New York City, I met this beautiful woman from the Netherlands. She was amazing, and I liked her. Yet was it the right decision for me to pursue her? I was praying at my church asking God if I should date this Dutch beauty when suddenly a man approached me who I did not know and had never seen before. He said to me,

"Your heart is in Europe. God is opening the doors of Europe for you. Your heart is in Europe."

I stood up and thought, "My heart is in Europe, and her name is Femke!"

I now realize that God was also speaking about my future ministry in Europe. This was just one of many confirmations that I had regarding my decision to pursue her and ask her to marry me. Not only am I very attracted to her, but everything that I ever wanted in a wife, partner, and in a mother for my children, I found in her.

We can trust God with every decision in our lives and know that many of the desires in our heart come from Him. "*Delight yourself in the LORD, and he will give you the desires of your heart*" (Psalm 37:4).

Creating the Future is the Job of Every Leader

In 1984, Reverend Henry Blackaby's association of churches in Vancouver decided that they were going to do a significant outreach to the visitors of the World's Fair Expo '86. There were only 2,000 members in all the churches, and the yearly income was around $9,000 that year. The churches decided they needed a working budget of $202,000 to do everything they felt God wanted them to do in 1986. At the end of that year, those churches had taken in over $264,000 for evangelistic outreaches.[61] They had created the future through the vision they received from God to do outreach.

It is responsibility of every leader to plan, budget, and in a very real sense *create* the future.

In Hebrews 6:5, there is an interesting phrase that says believers have *"tasted...the power of the age to come."* This speaks of us tapping into the future now. We bring heaven to earth through our lives and prayers. This is the essence of intercession when we pray as Jesus taught us to pray: *"Your kingdom come your will be done on earth as it is in heaven"* (Matt. 6:10). Our prayers can bring heaven to earth. As God said, *"Let there be light,"* and light existed, so our words can bring light into people's darkness (Genesis 1:3; Prov. 18:21).

Several years ago, a leader I know, was emotionally burned out and having a very difficult time functioning. However, her husband began to tell her, "You are going to get better and be a school teacher again. You are also going to teach at churches again about evangelism, Bible study, and other things you are passionate about."

She is now healthy and works as an elementary teacher. She regularly is a part of my prophetic teams and helps me teach schools of prophecy in churches as well. Her husband's words gave her hope, love, and life. He was creating the future with his words. When our heart lines up with God's heart, then we too can create hope, love, and life for others. Our words can help create the future.

Our words can help create the future.

The Scriptures are full of stories of prophets foreseeing things to prepare for the future. Agabus and Joseph both told of famines that were to come and that people needed to prepare for them (see Acts 11:28; Genesis 41:54). Hundreds of prophecies in the Old Testament described where Jesus would be born and how He would die hundreds of years before His birth (see Micah 5:2; Isaiah 53). This foretelling element of prophecy is very significant and important because it relates to planning, provision, and leading God's people. Nevertheless, this is not simply for prophets and pastors only, but for *every leader.*

I have always lived either with my mother or my wife. This means that I have always had someone who has taken care of buying groceries and cooking for me. In our first month of marriage, my wife told me that there was no food in the house that night as she left for work. I did not really believe her until I got hungry and could not find anything to eat. This was a wonderful lesson for me about foreseeing the future, which is another word for provision. Because I did not plan about food, I went hungry.

The prophet Amos speaks of a spiritual famine when he says: *"'The time is surely coming,' says the Sovereign Lord, 'when I will send a famine on the land—not a famine of bread or water but of hearing the words of the Lord. People will stagger from sea to sea and wander from border to border searching for the word of the Lord, but they will not find it'"* (Amos 8:11, 12).

In the Netherlands, there has been an interesting phenomenon of highly educated successful young people suffering from emotional burn-out.[62] Our secular Western European culture has decided we no longer need God and is suffering the spiritual, physical, and emotional consequences of this decision. A number of these young adults are searching for answers in yoga, mindfulness, meditation, and eastern religions. This is an opportunity for the Church to show spiritual fulfillment and human desire is found in knowing God through Jesus Christ.

Jesus said, *"Man shall not live by bread alone, but by every word that comes from the mouth of God"* (Matt 4:4).

When children are inside of their mother's wombs, they have an umbilical cord from which they get all their food from their mother. Knowing God is like learning to be attached to the Father heart of God through a metaphorical umbilical cord. Through prayer, meditation, Bible study, and fellowship we can know Him. Every believer needs to have their own spiritual umbilical cord where they get their own nutrition directly from heaven. Prophecy is simply sharing the heart and thoughts of God to people so that they can receive life-giving words from heaven.

There was a little boy who only had a few pieces of fish and bread in his lunch box. He gave them to Jesus, and more than five thousand people were fed from his small lunch (see John 6:1-14). A widow once had only one vial of oil, and the prophet Elijah helped turn that into many more (see 2 Kings 4). Making our plans together with God can provide for unexpected results. When we give God our words and resources, He can do so much more through them than we can by ourselves.

Years ago my brother asked a leader to pioneer a new church plant. In less than two weeks the leader was able to singlehandedly destroy the nascent church plant. I said, "Aaron, why did you do that? Why did you let that happen?

His answer was, "Matt, all we can do is do what we feel God wants us to do and leave the results in His hands."

We cannot judge immediate results as the determining factor of whether we have been obedient to God. Mary had to deliver her baby in a cow trough because there was no room for them in an Inn (see Luke 2: 6,7). Abraham had to wait until he was one hundred years old before Isaac was born (see Gen. 21:5). The scared disciples thought that everything was done and over with when they saw Jesus crucified on the cross (see John 20:19). Even after He was raised from the dead, they did not understand that the kingdom of God Jesus spoke of was not primarily a Jewish political kingdom, but a spiritual kingdom available for all people of all races (see Acts 1:6). God works in unexpected ways. When we partner with Him and His thoughts and words become our own, we can create the future.

God, I NEVER Want to Go to Amsterdam

When I was thirteen years old, a preacher came through our church in Oklahoma and started describing Amsterdam's Red-Light District as a dark and sinful place. He told us how scantily clad women stood behind the windows and that only mature and spiritually strong people should ever go serve people at places like that. His stories scared my thirteen-year-old imagination, and I recall thinking, "God, I will go to

Africa, South America, anywhere...but God I *never* want to go to Amsterdam."

Since 2005 I have lived in Amsterdam, and since 2016 I spend many hours every week visiting the people who work in Amsterdam's Red-Light District. God was preparing me then to do the kind of ministry we are currently doing. Often God prepares us for our future long before we are even aware of it. Moses was raised up in Pharaoh's palace so that he could eventually deliver the Israelites from Egypt (see Exodus 2). Saint Patrick became a beloved apostle to the Irish people who had formerly enslaved him. God was preparing me as a thirteen-year old for my assignment in Amsterdam's Red-Light District.

(It is now an honor to be able to help prostitutes in Amsterdam's Red Light District every week).

God can prepare us for future assignments in ways we would never humanly expect. It seems God does have a wise sense of humor.

Joseph's captivity and troubles, which appeared to be great evils, paved the way for God to preserve His people in a time of great famine. His whole family bowed to him as he had seen as a boy (see Genesis 50:20). We may not always have a complete description, but God can and will give us insight into the future when we step out and use our prophetic gift to speak forth His future.

The reason the Apostle Paul wrote the book of Romans was to ask for financial help to be able to go to Spain (see Romans 14:23-24). We do not know for sure whether Paul ever made it to Spain. We are, however, extremely indebted to him that he wrote the book of Romans.

We cannot foretell the future, but we can, together with God, be a part of *creating* it. As we pray and obey, we can expect God to do the unexpected.

Ecclesiastes 10:14b says, *"No one knows what is coming-- who can tell someone else what will happen after them?"* We cannot foretell the future in our own ability, but with God, we can be a part of *creating* it. As we pray and obey, we can expect God to do the unexpected. We can expect God to help us create the future.

Recently I got the following testimony from our ministry time in Budapest:

> "Hi Matt. I have a testimony for you. You prayed for me and gave me a prophecy in the prophetic conference a year ago. You told me that I was going to write books. I always had that desire in my heart, but after you said that to me I began considering it more seriously. Then during this year's prophetic conference, Jolande told me that I was going to write books for children.

> I want you to know that it is from God and that it is really happening. A publisher just offered me a contract and they will publish one of my fairy tales in a real book next month. I have other plans for publishing more books in the future. Thank you for your ministry and feel free to share this story with everyone you want to."

Prophetic ministry is never simply about telling the future, it is about getting connected to the one who holds the future in His hands. As we hold onto his hands, He enables us to create the future together with Him.

Prophetic ministry is never simply about telling the future, it is about getting connected to the one who holds the future in His hands.

Chapter 10

How To Make God's Love Tangible

"I died in 1973. My heart stopped.
I was brought before Jesus and he only asked me one thing:
Did you learn to love, Bob?" [63] -Prophet Bob Jones

On June 7, 1958, the Air National Guard's Minutemen were flying over Dayton, Ohio, drawing flowers and figures in the sky with puffs of smoke. Captain John Ferrier's plane lost control in the middle of the act. His plane was flying dangerously toward the town of Fairborn. Ferrier did not respond to his colleague on the radio, but instead gave small bursts of smoke before his plane crashed.

Ferrier had remained in his plane and managed to crash it in a garden between four homes. The witnesses realized that no one perished, except for Ferrier, because he had given his life to save theirs. A few days later, his wife, Tulle, extracted a card from his wallet that read, "I am third. God is first. Others are second, and I am third." Ferrier did not just talk about his faith, he lived his faith out even in the way that he sacrificed his life for others.[64]

The Kingdom of God is about power and not just about words (see 1 Cor. 4:20). In this chapter, I endeavor to provide values or keys so we can make God's love and power more tangible to people. Remember, the focus of every spiritual gift is not to show off, nor is it for our exclusive benefit; it is to reach out to a lost and dying world with the love and power of Jesus Christ. Just as every prophetic word is to lift up, encourage, and point toward Jesus, we reach the lost by making His love real and tangible to hurting people.

Evangelism and prophecy are first and foremost not something we *do* but something that we *are*. If the Gospel is at the core of my identity, it is easy and normal to share my faith with others. If God is my best friend, then it is normal and easy to prophesy. It is easy to tell others what God want to say to them.

> If God is my best friend, then it is normal and easy to prophesy.

In their book *The Tangible Kingdom,* Hugh Halter and Matt Smay speak of three dimensions of spiritual life that can help us experience God. They are: Communion with God, Community with other believers, and Mission to the world. I like to describe them as the Upward, Inward, and Outward dimensions of living out our faith. Leaving out one of these dimensions will lead to unbalanced growth. Just like a body builder who only works on his upper body, and not on his lower body, so our spiritual life will be warped and unbalanced if we leave out one of these dimensions. Here is a description of these dimensions of holistic spirituality.

Upward, Inward, and Outward

The Upward dimension consists of a person's devotional relationship with God. Inward consists of the discipleship relationships a person has with other believers. Outward is the relationships cultivated with people who are not believers (yet). Halter and Smay, together with other believers, came up with the following diagram to illustrate when God's love becomes tangible.

Their goal was to see how the Kingdom of God could be practically fleshed out (incarnated) in communities of believers. They concluded that when all three of these areas (Up, In, and Out) come together: God's love is tangible.

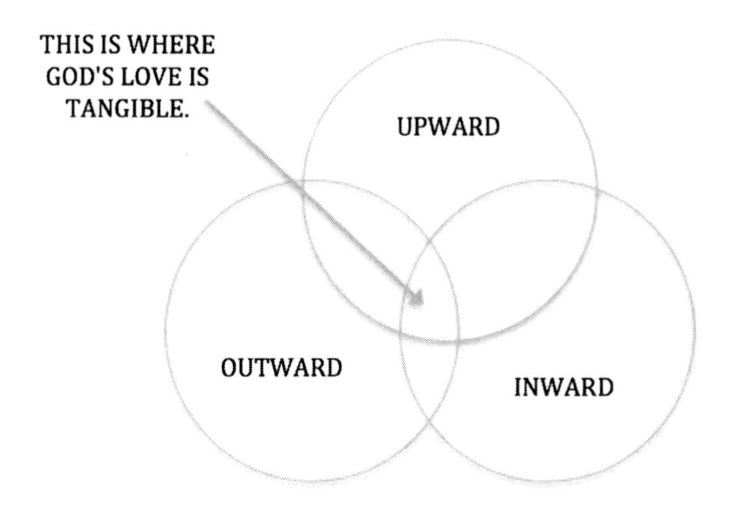

The Upward Relationship with God

"I am the vine; and you are the branches. If you remain in me and I in you, you will bear much fruit; apart from me you can do nothing." –Jesus (John 15:5)

This is the most important dimension of Church life. It is an upward and downward dynamic of us speaking to God and Him speaking to us. As we speak to Him and cultivate our secret life, He interacts with us. He helps us with every other area and dimension of our lives.

The Inward Relationship with Other Believers

"Our time, effort, energy and focus must be on how the Gospel is spread and how disciples are being made...It's a lot easier to build buildings, fill them up, and have special events than it is to pour into the lives of people and make multiplying disciples. But it is the only thing that will really work." *–Bob Roberts Jr.*[65]

Disciples are the people in whom we invest our time and mentor. We should also search for people who can mentor us in whatever we want to grow in. Church is not just a service we attend, it is a family we belong to. Being able to be vulnerable, honest, and open to one another is important.

Leadership is all about helping people develop to their highest potential. Jesus taught that leadership is leaders serving followers and not follower serving leaders. Many believers do not have anyone mentoring them or people whom they are mentoring. Discipleship is vital and works best when combined with the other two dimensions.

Neil Cole's *Life Transformation Group* is my favorite discipleship method. Gender-specific small groups get together for discipleship and to answer accountability questions, discuss Scripture, and pray for the lost. These three activities correspond to the Upward, Inward and Outward dimensions of discipleship. [66] He articulates the three dimensions with the letters D.N.A.

"D" stands for "Divine Truth," which each person engages is through reading Scripture. "N" stands for "Nurturing Relationships," which deals with being vulnerable, transparent, and authentic when going through the accountability questions. "A" is for "Apostolic Mission," which is the emphasis upon praying for people who do not believe in Christ yet. [67] Cole describes these three dimensions of spiritual life with different words, but with the same meaning.

The Outward Relationship with the World

"Jesus was not crucified in a cathedral between two candles, but on a cross between two thieves—on the town heap, at the crossroads—so cosmopolitan they had to write His title in Hebrew and Latin and Greek. The Son of God was crucified at the kind of place where cynics talk smut, where thieves curse, and where soldiers gamble. Because that is where He died and since that is what He died for, that is where

Christians can best share His message of love because that is what real Christianity is all about." – George Macleod[68]

Many churches may be good at one or two of these dimensions, yet this third outreach often lacks. This is reaching out to people that are not believers. Jesus came *"to seek and to save the lost"* (Luke 19:10).

I see these three dimensions come together at places such as psychic fairs or in the Red-Light District. These are not places Christians normally frequent, yet I do see God's love and power become very real in such places. We should not be afraid of the world, but we should love the world the same way that Christ loves us. I actually prefer being in the Red-Light District when it is dark because that is when God's light in me shines the brightest. Light is stronger than darkness, and His love is greater than fear. As C.T. Studd once said, "Some wish to live within the sound of a chapel bell. I want to run a rescue mission within a yard of hell."[69]

Let's look at some keys to this Outward dynamic from Luke chapter seven.

Key #1: "Create a Culture of Honor

"When Jesus had finished saying all this to the people who were listening, he entered Capernaum" (Luke 7:1)

Another leader we can learn from about making God's love and power tangible is a Roman military leader in Scripture who models some of the key values to make God's love and power tangible (see Luke 7:1-10). As he could tap into the love and power of Jesus then, so we can tap into it today.

The name Capernaum means the village of Nahum or the village of comfort. The Prophet Isaiah prophesied about this region in chapter nine of his book. He spoke about a great light shining in the darkness and honor replacing shame (see Isaiah 9:1-2). God makes Himself known in dark places. Where sin abounds, His grace increases even more (see Romans 5:20). Simon Peter, Andrew, James, John, and Matthew all came from Capernaum. That's five of Jesus' twelve disciples. It was also the city where Jesus did many of His miracles and the supernatural was natural.

A goal of ministry is to raise up spiritual sons and daughters who will form new communities—places where making God's love and power tangible is common, normal, and natural. This takes place best in an atmosphere where people love and care for one another. Such places are ideal to help people learn how to become more like Jesus.

In my eighth grade year of school, I had a basketball coach named Chris Busch. He not only taught me how to shoot a basketball, he also believed in me as an individual. To this day, I call him "coach" and have breakfast with him whenever I am in Tulsa. He is a mentor who showed me that valuing and treasuring people is the most important thing we can do. He honored me as a person and not because of how well I could shoot a ball.

> Valuing and treasuring people is the most important thing we can do.

In the previous chapter, I mentioned that the name God gave Himself was "I Am that I Am" and not "I do what I do" (Exodus 3:14). Our worth should not be in what we do, but in who we are—and this is true for everyone. We are all made in the image of God, and every human has inherent value (see Genesis 1:26-28). No matter what a person believes or does, they are valuable.

Jesus does not invite only people whose lives are in perfect order to come to Him. He says, *"Come to me all you who are weary and heavy burdened and I will give you rest"* (Matthew 11:28).

In the Netherlands it is not common to compliment one another. At a grocery store in the Netherlands there was a sign that said, "We like to give compliments." It was a way of being able to ask young people for their ID to see how old they were when they buy cigarettes or alcohol. I would always take advantage of this sign and ask for a compliment. I never got one, but I always asked God for a compliment to give the cashier. Our words should honor people and add to people's lives and not take value away.

Key #2: Make Caring For the Sick, Poor and Vulnerable a Priority

"There a centurion's servant, whom his master valued highly, was sick and about to die" (Luke 7:2).

"I can't do this anymore. You wait here, I will be back." These were the last words the twelve-year-old Bill heard from his mother as she abandoned him on a park bench. Three days later, he still sat on that same bench not knowing what to do.

Dave, a Christian mechanic, saw him sitting there and decided to help him. He helped him find a place to stay and paid for him to go to a Christian camp. That little boy grew up to establish an international children's ministry that today reaches thousands of street children. Bill Wilson has become an advocate for the poor and inner-city children around the world.[70] Bill Wilson makes the love and power of God tangible.

After graduating from college, I wanted to go somewhere where people did not just talk about God, but did what He told us to do. Getting to live and work in the inner city of New York was a life-changing experience. I got to serve the poor children of the inner city not only words, but with deeds.

Visiting children who lived in the projects in the Bronx as well as teaching them God's word was awesome. I don't ever want to be a hearer of God's words and not a doer. I refuse to be a comfortable arm chair theologian who can talk good, but does not live out what he believes. It is vital that we make practically applying God's instructions a priority.

An important part of church ministry is caring for the sick and the poor. When we care for the hungry, the naked, the sick, the imprisoned, and refugees, we are taking care of *Jesus* (see Matt. 25). Being generous to the poor is as valuable and important as prayer itself (see Acts 10:1-5). This is why I have set up a foundation to help fight poverty in third world nations (www.feedpeople.eu). It is important that we take care of the poor in our own neighborhoods and cities as well as in other parts of the world. The ministry of healing and caring for the poor is as relevant now as it was two thousand years ago!

Key #3: Make Praying for Physical and Inner Healing Normal

"The centurion heard of Jesus and sent some elders of the Jews to him, asking him to come and heal his servant." (Luke 7:3)

The most loving thing we can do for people is to bring them to Jesus through prayer. We only pray about the things that we care about. Praying for people is a high act of love and care. Do not worry about whether someone will get healed or not when you pray. Pray for them full of faith so that whether they get healed or not, they will know that you and God loves them.

Praying for physical and emotional healing are both very important. Model transparency and authenticity so that people can find healing for their brokenness. People have told me about secrets they never dared to tell anyone. This helped them find healing and closure to issues they were never able to deal with alone.

One leader warned me that I was never to tell any of my weaknesses to any of the people in my church. I disagree. Make it normal to not only tell the stories, but also times of blunders and mistakes. This gives us more credibility and authority to our listeners as well as keeping us humble. It is good to know that we are all human.

Key #4: Be Sensitive and Gracious to People of Other Cultures and Faiths

"When they came to Jesus, they pleaded earnestly with him, 'This man deserves to have you do this, because he loves our nation and has built our synagogue.' So Jesus went with them. He was not far from the house when the centurion sent friends to say to him: 'Lord don't trouble yourself, for I do not deserve to have you come under my roof. That is why I did not even consider myself worthy to come to you.'" (Luke 7:4-7a)

The Roman centurion built a synagogue from his own resources for the Jews. This would be an investment of hundreds of thousands or millions of dollars in today's money. I make it a point to honor people of other faiths or of no faith when I speak from a pulpit. I attempt to spend time with people who are not Christians so that I can value them and learn how they think. Spending time with people of different perspectives helps me not insulate myself in a Christian bubble.

Spending time with people of different perspectives helps me not insulate myself in a Christian bubble.

During Ramadan, Islam's time of fasting, we get to eat with our Muslim neighbors as they break their fast. Not only do we get to enjoy a meal, we get to spend time with people who often see God and life differently than we do. We may not agree in everything, but we can honor and value one another. This helps us learn and grow from other people. It also enables us to communicate the values in our hearts more effectively to them. Honoring and valuing people of different backgrounds is very important. Reaching out to people different that ourselves is a great way of growing and learning.

The Roman centurion was being sensitive to the Jewishness of Jesus when he asked him not to come into his home. Jews were not allowed to go into the homes of gentiles. The centurion did not want Jesus to break His own religious laws. He went out of his way to serve the cultural sensitivities of Jesus. This would be like cooking kosher or halal food when eating with a Jewish or Muslim friend today. Respect and cultural sensitivity can go a long way in being able to share God's love with others.

Missionary Frank Laubach had a life-changing experience in Mindanao, Philippines, in 1929. There he did an experiment with God to see if he could stay in contact with Him. At one point, he began to speak as if it was God speaking through him. These were the words which came out:

"My Child, you have failed because you do not really love these Moros. You feel superior to them because you are white. If you can forget you are an American and think only how I love them, they will respond." Laubach went on to say, "After that night on Signal Hill, when God killed my racial prejudice and made me color-blind, it seemed as though He was working miracles at every turn."

Laubach began spending a lot of time with the Muslim leaders and people of the village. After two years, he could not believe the results of his work. He said, "I do nothing I can see excepting to pray for them, and to walk among them thinking of God. They know I am a Protestant. Yet two of the leading Moslem priests have gone around the province telling everybody that I would help the people to know God."[71]

Laubach was able to reach the people of that Philippine island. He also created a literacy method that helped more than sixty million people learn to read and write. God can do miracles when we reach out to people who are different than ourselves. This was true for Laubach and the Roman centurion.

Key #5: Expect the Words of Jesus to Change Lives

"But say the word, and my servant will be healed." (Luke 7:7b)

The centurion was unaware that he was speaking to the very Word of God Himself. Jesus created heaven and earth in the beginning (see John 1:1-3). "God said, *'Let there be light,'* and there was light" (Genesis 1:3). The power that spoke things into existence is available to us today. It is the same power that raised Jesus from the dead (see Ephesians 1:19-20).

God created the world through speech. Jesus walked on water, turned water into wine, raised the dead, and did miracles. If He did this then, we can expect Him to do miracles today.

Prophetic ministry is tapping into the creative power of the spoken Word of God. His words are dynamic and full of life. God's words are like a weaver's machine. He can take the tapestry of people's broken lives and can make them whole again. He can turn all things, even evil ones, into good (see Rom. 8:28 and Gen. 50:20).

Phil Strout, the national leader of the Vineyard Association of churches, has said "Without God's presence we have no power; without the proclamation, we really don't make a difference, and without things practical we never get traction or movement."[72] Expect the spoken word of God to make a difference in people's lives in practical and tangible ways that will give new life.

Key #6: Understand How Spiritual Authority and Power Works

"For I myself am a man under authority, with soldiers under me. I tell this one, 'Go,' and he goes; and that one, 'Come,' and he comes. I say to my servant, 'Do this,' and he does it. When Jesus heard this, he was amazed at him and turning to the crowd following him, he said, "I tell you, I have not found such great faith even in Israel." (Luke 7:8-9)

To be a good leader, we must be good followers. Anyone who is unable to follow is also unable to lead others. The centurion knew that in his sphere of influence, he could tell those under him what to do. He also recognized that Jesus operated from a greater sphere of influence than his own. The centurion wisely submitted himself and his servant to the authority of Jesus. This allowed Jesus to bring healing to his servant.

Individual freedom is the highest value in the Netherlands. It is common for me to hear people say, "I believe in God, but in my own way."

What they mean is, "I am in the one in charge of my life and I can think and do whatever I want. No one can tell me what to do or think."

Although this may be true, it is ineffective in the Kingdom of God. A paradox of the Kingdom of God is that freedom is living under the authority of Jesus Christ. Jesus said, *"For whoever wants to save their life will lose it, but whoever loses their life for me will find it"* (Matthew 16:25). True freedom is knowing that my life is not my own, but that it belongs to Jesus (see Gal. 2:20). We get authority from Jesus to speak into people's lives by being under His authority. His leadership in our lives leads to freedom and not bondage.

"Power is the ability, the strength, the might to complete a given task. Authority is the right to use the power of God."[73] Authority is more like a police officer stopping a car by waving his arm or turning his lights on. Jesus Christ has all authority in heaven and earth, and He wants *us* to use it (see Matt. 28:18-20; Luke 10:19-20).

We can only use His authority when we are under His leadership. Freedom is having every area of our lives (relationships, finances, sexuality, etc.) under the authority of Jesus Christ. When we give Him the keys to our hearts, He can bring life and order to every area of our lives.

Healing came to the home of the centurion because he trusted and submitted to Jesus. Submitting our lives to Christ is the best way to find freedom and healing.

Key #6: Record, Celebrate and Publish God's Miracles

"Then the men who had been sent returned to the house and found the servant well" (Luke 7:10).

In 2010 at a church in Oklahoma City, an aunt of a young man asked me if we could pray for her nephew, who was not present. I prayed for him by laying my hands on her and then went on with my sermon. Five minutes later, the pastor interrupted my sermon with a text message from the boy's mother. She said that five minutes earlier her son's ears had popped open. The faith level in the room shot up and God made himself known in a very special way that evening!

Whenever possible, have healings and miracles medically verified. It is important that we testify of what God does as well as avoid telling stories that never took place. This takes effort and follow up, yet testimonies of healings and life change are valuable. They help build up faith and help us praise God for all that he has done and will continue doing.

> It is important that we testify of what God does as well as avoid telling stories that never took place.

In Exodus 16:34, Moses tells the Israelites to keep a jar of manna for future generations to see how God fed them. After crossing the Jordan River, Joshua had a memorial built to commemorate how God opened it (see Joshua 4). Record miracles, because we can forget what God has done and what He still wants to do in our lives. I enjoy reading church history and seeing what God has done in the past. It fills me with faith to ask God to do similar things in my lifetime.

Key #7 Make Supernatural Ministry Natural and Normal for Everybody

Just as Jesus was accessible to the centurion, He is accessible to everyone now. He is the one who desires to speak to us and be our friend (see Rev. 3:20). Sometimes I take children and teenagers to be my ministry team when I speak in churches. I will never forget when a nine-year old girl prayed for a woman who had no feeling in her toes. She walked up to her and said, "Jesus, will you be with her toes." The feeling came into her toes after that simple prayer.

After healing a paralytic, Peter said, *"Fellow Israelites, why does this surprise you? Why do you stare at us as if by our own power or godliness we had made this man walk?"* (Acts 3:12).

It is not our godliness that enables us to make the love and power of God tangible to people around us. It is accessible and available to everyone through Jesus.

A preacher once asked the famous healing evangelist T.L. Osborne, "Is there a price to be paid to be used by God in the healing ministry?" His response was, "Yes! There is a very high price to be paid," but immediately followed with, "But Jesus paid it all on the cross!" [74]

The ability to make God's love and power tangible is available to everyone.

Key #8 People Remember What You Say and Do

"Let the women, children and unsaved into the lifeboats." -John Harper, April 14, 1912 on the *Titanic*[75]

John Harper was on his way from Scotland to preach in Chicago when the *Titanic* began sinking. He took his little daughter to a lifeboat and there began saying, "Let the women, children and unsaved into the lifeboats."

John Harper gave his lifejacket to someone else knowing that he probably was going to die. When he was in the frigid waters, survivors told how he swam to people saying, "Believe in the Lord Jesus Christ and thou shalt be saved."

One Scottish young man recalled him coming to him and asking him if he was saved. He responded, "No."

Harper drifted away from the young man, but the currents would bring them back together for Harper's last moment of breath.

Again, Harper asked the young man if he wanted to be saved. Then he took a last breath and shouted at the top of his lungs, "Believe in the Lord Jesus Christ and thou shalt be saved."

The young man decided to believe in Christ after he saw Harper disappear and drown in the Atlantic Ocean.

Harper's faith was real. He did not just talk about the love and power of God, he lived it. To make God's love and power tangible, *we can't just talk about it, we must live it.*

Bringing It All Together

When I first moved to the Netherlands, I wanted to find practical way to make God's love tangible. In fact, the mission of the church we planted in Amsterdam is to "Make God's love tangible." [76] We felt this can be accomplished by serving people with practical acts of service and by using the gifts of the Holy Spirit.

Sometimes, instead of having a church service, we find practical ways to serve our neighborhood. This may be by doing things as simple as cleaning up the street or handing out flowers that our neighbors can plant.

We also plan times when we will intentionally use the gifts of the Holy Spirit such as during psychic fairs, healing services, prophetic evenings or during large public holiday such as the Dutch King's birthday. It is so fun and often easier to share the message of Jesus after someone has been healed or we have perfectly described a situation in their life without even knowing them personally. This allows them to see that God not only exists, but that He cares and knows about every area of their lives.

Unfortunately, creating a culture where God's love and power becomes tangible does not simply just "happen." We need to make an effort in planning and creating moments where people can experience God. To facilitate this, we use the Upward, Inward, and Outward concepts to help us remember to keep our vertical relationship with God fresh, to be discipling others within our sphere of influence, and to be reaching out to the lost with the love of Jesus.

Operating in the gifts of the Spirit, such as prophecy, words of knowledge, and healing, will often open people's lives to receive from God. We do not heal someone or tell them things about their lives to show off or perform a parlor trick; we do so because God often uses His power to breach the walls so many have created around their hearts. When He makes an opening, they are often more receptive to the love of God. When people experience God's love tangibly through supernatural gifts, this can help them come to know Jesus Christ.

Jolande Bijl, who mentored me in doing ministry at psychic fairs, told me a story once that illustrates this point.

During a public demonstration at a psychic fair of the "supernatural power of love," she asked a woman if she could give her a personal word from Jesus Christ. As she began to prophesy over her, the woman said that nothing she was saying was true. Bijl simply said,

"Well, that is what I heard Jesus say. If you want to talk to me afterwards at my table, I am available."

After the public demonstration, the woman appeared at her table. She told Bijl the following story: "Before your demonstration, a psychic had told everybody all kinds of details about my life and publicly mocked me and made me feel terrible. When you began speaking over my life, I was afraid that you were going to do the same. Instead, you spoke about the greatest desires of my heart and honored me. What should I do next?"

Bijl then led this woman in a prayer to ask Jesus to come into her life and has since become a member of a local church. That day she encountered the love of Jesus tangibly and it changed her life forever. It was changed because a believer dared to make God's love and power tangible at a place known for witchcraft, tarot cards, magic and psychics.

Jesus came to seek and to save that which was lost (see Luke 19:10). He did this while cultivating an intimate relationship with His father and with His disciples (see John 14:10-14). We too are called to tap into the power of God to make the love of God tangible to everyone around us.

Chapter 11
How to Heal the Sick

"Heal the sick, raise the dead, cleanse those who have leprosy, drive out demons. Freely you have received; freely give." (Matthew 10:7-8)

(Demonstrating healing at a youth conference.)

Every year around my birthday, my mother tells the dramatic and miraculous story of my birth. I was born in Concepcion, Chile. The doctors said I was dying and needed to be delivered immediately. They were able to get us to the only hospital with incubators, because the doctors did not know if I was going to survive without one.

Once in the hospital, the doctor gave my mother anesthesia so she wouldn't feel the operation. Unfortunately, they gave her too much. After pulling me out of my mother's womb, she stopped breathing.

They got her breathing again, but instead of watching her, they left her in the hall way all alone!

My mother is a nurse and knew it was very likely she would stop breathing again. The only nurse who came by told her, her baby boy was going to die. As she lay there, she begin to pray Psalm 23 where it says, *"Yeah, though I walk through the valley of the shadow of death I will fear no evil for you are with me."*

She recalls the feeling of a black cloud coming down as a darkness of fear and death. She was fighting for her own life and the life of her baby (me)! As she prayed, she asked God to have other people praying for her at that moment. She felt like we were not going to make it.

Six months later, a friend of hers who lived in Alaska asked my mother what happened on January 12th. This friend said on that date, she awakened with a sudden urge to pray for us. She had no idea what was going on, but somehow, this woman was made aware we needed prayer. God used the prayers of a woman in Alaska to save our lives!

The story does not stop there. My parents brought home a very sick child. The doctors later diagnosed me with Cerebral Palsy and let them know I would never walk or talk. Cerebral Palsy is incurable. The doctors prepared my parents for what life would look like taking care of a child with CP. Every day my parents did exercises with my little limbs.

My parents loved me and knew they were going to care for me no matter what. They believed in the power of prayer. They believed God still does miracles today.

One of the people who was praying for me was my Aunt Candy in California. She had a weekly women's prayer meeting that got together every Thursday. They did what the Apostle Paul did in Acts 19:11-12 and mailed an anointed prayer cloth (actually a tissue) to my mother in Chile. My mother sewed the cloth onto my pajamas. One month later, all effects of Cerebral Palsy were gone from my little body!

When we returned to the United States six months later, doctors could not tell that I was ever afflicted with the sickness. It was a miracle, or can I dare to say, *I am a living miracle*! I know without a doubt that healing is for today, because I have personally experienced it

Jesus Still Heals Today

(With Iskander sharing God's love and power in down town Amsterdam.)

In 2015, I took Iskander, a young 20-year-old Dutch man, to the streets of Amsterdam to pray for people to be healed. That first day, three people were completely or partially healed after we prayed for them. He was so excited that he joined another friend and started seeing people healed in Amsterdam daily. Eventually, we started going once a week to the streets to pray for strangers.

One week, he told me, "Matt, I am going to pray for people with crutches and believe that they are going to be healed."

The next week, he told me that he had seen his first person with crutches healed. On that same day, we also saw a young Spanish boy healed and able to walk without his crutch anymore.

It was then that he told me, "Matt, now I am going for people in wheelchairs."

The next week, he told me he had seen the first person in a wheelchair healed so that they could stand up and walk. It was awesome!

Then he went to a large Dutch Christian conference to be part of the prayer team to pray for the sick (Opwekking 2016). He stood at the wheelchair section and kept praying for people in wheelchairs. Three people in wheelchairs were healed that weekend! One of them was Marije de Vries.

Marije had an operation due to a bone that was growing out of the side of her foot. Because of the malformation of her foot, she had had pain in her back and hips all throughout her life. Now that she was finally old enough for the operation, she had decided to have it done.

The doctors cut and pasted different bones and tendons to her foot so that she would be able to walk normally. The recovery time was supposed to be at least three months, and she would have pain for at least a year.

When she attended the conference, it had been a month since the operation, and Marije found herself asking God for healing. Iskander, along with others, repeatedly prayed for her Friday, Saturday, and Sunday. However, instead of the pain becoming less, it became *greater*. It only got worse when she slipped and fell on it. However, she was determined to not stop praying for her complete healing.

Monday, she refused to go home before she was prayed for again. She found Iskander and another young man and asked them to pray for her once more. The two prayed for her repeatedly until the healing started taking place.[77] Marije went from having severe constant pain to being able to run while pushing her wheelchair without any pain!

Unfortunately, Marije still had to wait two weeks before her cast could be removed. However, the doctors were astounded when they removed the cast. Her foot was completely healed and she was free to do whatever she wanted!

(Picture with Marije and her foot after having the cast replaced.)

Marije's healing illustrates the importance of not giving up when praying for people's healing. If Marije had given up after receiving prayer on Friday, Saturday, and Sunday, then she may have not been healed on Monday. Perseverance in prayer is necessary for everyone who wants to see people get healed through prayer.

Persevering in Prayer for Healing

John Wimber[78] felt God told him to pray for the sick at his church in Anaheim, California. For the next ten months, no one got healed after receiving prayer. In fact, the people praying for healing were getting sick themselves after praying for others. Wimber wanted to stop, but God did not let him. After ten months of faithfully praying for healing, he saw the first healing. That was the beginning of a healing ministry that helped launch the Vineyard movement of churches. His ministry affected many other denominations and movements around the world.

After Todd White[79] was dramatically delivered from a life of crime and drug addiction, he discovered divine healing. For three and a half months he prayed for ten people a day to be healed. Wherever he was at (supermarkets, gas stations, work, etc.) he would pray for people to be healed. After having prayed for more than nine hundred people for healing, he finally saw the first healing take place. Now White is seeing healings every day as God gives him words of knowledge everywhere he goes.

Jordan Seng describes his struggle with healing ministry in his book *Miracle Work.*

> If you believe God enables you to perform supernatural feats, you'll sometimes feel terrible when you fail. At our church's healing services, roughly half of those who come for ministry receive at least partial physical healing during the service. Many experience progressive healing afterward, and about 15 percent receive total and immediate healing during the service itself. We register about a 10 percent success rate even with ostensibly incurable diseases. We seem to have an almost perfect success rate with some diseases, and our breakthrough rate for deliverance ministry is also quite high. We're in no way approaching Jesus' level of power and effectiveness, but I guess you could say there's cause for encouragement. Yet when we fail to heal a beautiful little girl with leukemia or a young mom with brain tumors, we feel the bite, and almost always wonder if we should have done better.[80]

I grew up watching my father, Dean, pray for thousands of people who were healed of many kinds of sicknesses. He wrote to me about some of the joys, but also frustrations, of praying for the sick. Here are some of the experiences he shared:

> In a service in Tomé (Chile), I prayed five successive nights for a 15-year-old with no hip socket who limped badly. As he limped away from the prayer line that last night of services, I

felt like crawling down a hole! I had prayed my best and my hardest and nothing had happened.

I decided to hide my feelings of disappointment and continue praying for the sick, but without testing the rest to see if they were healed. A lady brought up her little 18-month-old boy for prayer. I asked her what his problem was, and she said that he had the same problem as that 15-year-old: no hip socket from birth. (My faith for this healing was now very low).

A few minutes later, the congregation started cheering. I learned that the little boy had gotten a new hip socket when I prayed for him and was walking down the aisle and with no limp at all! Many of his relatives came to faith because of this healing.

Still, I was disturbed. Why did God heal him and not the 15-year-old?

Finally, I had enough! I told the Lord I was through praying for the sick. I would preach the Gospel so people would "get saved," but I just couldn't take all of the embarrassing failures when I prayed for them! I would even stop fasting and praying before the meetings!

In the next meeting I preached, people came up to give their lives to the Lord. I sat down, smugly thinking I was done. That's when the pastor got up and announced to the congregation: "Brother Dean is now going to pray for the sick!"

Boy was I mad! I told the Lord, "No. You can't do this to me! I can't take being disappointed again by praying for severe cases and not seeing them healed."

However, I didn't want to embarrass the pastor, so I got up and started laying hands on the people one-by-one.

Amazing healings started taking place. A girl who could not lift her right arm could lift it above her head. A girl with a blind eye could suddenly see perfectly. More healings took place, and I had not even prayed and fasted before the service!

After the service, I repented. I told the Lord no matter how embarrassed I got, I would keep on praying for the sick. I would obey His commandment to heal the sick no matter how weak my faith might be or disappointed I could feel. I have never regretted that decision!

(I watched my dad see thousands of people's backs healed when he commanded a leg to grow and become equal with the other one. Now I teach others to pray for the sick as my father taught me.)

Healing the Sick is a "Normal" Part of Following Jesus

I have been in services where it seemed like nearly everybody I prayed for experienced healing in their bodies. I have also been at services where nobody experienced healing when I prayed for them.

Not everyone we pray for gets healed, but no one will get healed if we *do not* pray.

Not everyone we pray for gets healed, but no one will get healed if we *do not* pray.

The same principle regarding praying for the sick is true concerning sharing our faith. Not everyone I share my faith with will become a Christian, yet I should never allow that to impede me from sharing my faith. Sharing my faith and praying for healing are acts of love. My goal is that no matter what may or may not happen, people know I (and God) love them. For God, nothing is impossible when we share our faith and pray.

In 2010, I saw several deaf ears pop open. Later that year, I met a deaf man at a park in Amsterdam. I prayed for him, but he was not healed. However, when I finished praying, he did have a tear in his eye and he thanked me that I cared enough to pray and ask God to heal him. Our job is to lovingly pray for healing and leave the results in God's hands.

God heals people, we don't. Relax and pray for healing in a manner that people will feel honored and loved no matter what. The more you pray for the sick to be healed, the more healings you will see. The more people are praying for the sick, the more people will get healed. Don't stop praying for the sick.

Jesus commanded us to heal the sick (see Matt. 10:8). Just as we should give to the poor, pray for our enemies and forgive people, so we should make it a practice of praying for the sick. Jesus and Paul describe healing, signs and wonders, as being a vital part of sharing our faith (Mark 16:17-18 and Rom. 15:17-20). Healing the sick is a normal part of following Jesus.

How To Pray for Healing: A Five-Step Model

My brother Aaron was once asked to come up with a model to train Brazilian teenagers to pray for the sick. He came up with these five steps to pray for healing. Thousands of healings have taken place using these steps. Here are five steps you may follow if you want to heal the sick:

Step 1: When Appropriate, Place Your Hands on Area(s) of Sickness.

"They will be able to place their hands on the sick, and they will be healed" (Mark 16: 18c)

When praying for sick, always ask for permission before you lay your hands on a person. If it is inappropriate to place your hand where they are sick, place your hand on their head or their shoulder. Never push someone or place your weight on them! If it is inappropriate to lay a hand on someone, but they allow you to pray, do it. It is not about following a model but giving space to God to do a miracle.

Step 2: Command the Body Part to Be Healed.

"Jesus reached out and touched him. 'I am willing,' he said. 'Be healed!' And instantly the leprosy disappeared" (Matt. 8:3)

Jesus never asked the Father to heal the sick. He always commanded the sick to be healed. Jesus has all authority, and He has given this authority to us to cast out demons and to heal the sick (see Matt. 28:18; 10:1). He modeled for us that praying for healing is not a request, but a command based on the own spiritual authority Jesus has given to us.

Step 3: Command Any Spirits of Sickness to Leave

Some sicknesses (not all) are caused by demons. In Luke 13:10-13 we read about a woman Jesus healed who was crippled by a spirit for eighteen years. It is useful to pray, *"If there is any spirit of sickness present, I command you to leave."*

A possible sign of demonic activity is when the pain in their body starts moving around when you start commanding it to leave. If you discern that there is spiritual activity going on, don't stop praying until you feel that the job is complete. Do not be intimidated.

Step 4: Ask Them to Try What They Could not Do.

"On another Sabbath he went into the synagogue and was teaching, and a man was there whose right hand was shriveled.... He looked around at them all, and then said to the man, 'Stretch out your hand.' He did so, and his hand was completely restored." (Luke 6:6, 10)

At times, a person does not realize they are healed until they start testing themselves. This means if a person suffers from back pain or neck pain, I will ask them to bend over or look to their right and left. Avoid them hurting themselves doing this, but often this act of faith *releases* healing.

My father prayed once for a man whose foot was bent completely to the left. He told him to do a kicking movement, and the third time he kicked, his foot straightened out!

Marleen Kleppees suffered from Cerebral Palsey (the same disease I was born with). During prayer one day she had a vision where Jesus told her she was going to be healed. She called a local church and asked them to pray for her. The pastor prayed for her and then asked her to by faith get out of the wheel chair and begin walking. She got up and started running around the church. She was completely healed. The step of faith to get out of the wheel chair was part of the process God used to heal her. [81]

It is important that people get themselves checked out by a doctor. If they are on medications, they should not cease immediately. If they are healed, the doctor will be able to verify this. Just as Jesus sent the lepers to the temple to be checked if they were cleansed, so we should have ourselves checked out to verify healings.

Verifying and documenting healings when possible with a doctor is a great way to testify of the veracity that Jesus still heals today.

Step 5: Evaluate Results, and If Necessary, Repeat Steps 1-4

Jesus had to pray for a blind man twice before he was totally healed (see Mark 8:23-25). If Jesus had to pray twice for someone's healing, I may need to pray twenty times. Healing is often a *process* instead of instantaneous. If a person is not completely healed after praying once, keep on praying! As long as the person is engaged and you find it appropriate, keep praying.

One woman who attended our church was healed of fibromyalgia after praying for her for over three years. Every time that we prayed for her, she felt partially better. Nevertheless, one day she forgave someone and was completely healed after we prayed. Healing is often a process, so do not give up after praying once.

Have the courage to ask a person, "So how are you feeling now?" Rate their pain on a scale of 0-10 (10 being a lot pain and 0 being totally gone). Celebrate every time the pain has gone lower on the scale, and keep praying believing for a zero.

Also, you don't need to pray long and with too many words. When praying for strangers on the street, I pray short prayers so that I can pray two or three times if possible. It is not the length of your prayer that creates the miracle.

In Bunschoten, the Netherlands, I shared these five steps to pray for healing during a Sunday morning service. A man received prayer eight times in a row before his chronic stomachache disappeared. He has not suffered from that pain since. It was good that his friend did not stop praying after the seventh time.

Do People Have to Have Faith to Be Healed?

The short answer is no. In Europe, relatively few people believe in God, and yet I see quite a few healings on the streets when I pray for unbelievers. Our job is simply to pray and believe and trust God no matter what. We should never blame people if they do not have enough faith or they do not get healed. That is not helpful at all. Instead, make it your goal that whether or not they do get healed, they will be thankful you cared enough to pray for them.

> Make it your goal that whether or not they do get healed, they will be thankful you cared enough to pray for them.

Does My Faith Have to be High To Heal the Sick

The short answer is also no. John Wimber told this story which illustrated the principle that people's healings do not depend on us being at the right place with the right attitude and at the right time.

"I remember standing at a urinal in an airport in Phoenix. A guy leaned over and put his face in front of mine and said, 'You're him, aren't you?' He wanted to shake hands with me. I said, 'I'm a little busy right now.' He said, 'Will you pray for me?' I said, 'Before or after I wash my hands?' This actually happened! I could not believe it!"

"So, I washed my hands and prayed for him."

"I heard through a friend of his that he was healed...Right at that moment all I had was anger. I never felt so put off in my life! It certainly wasn't my faith, but I did do what Jesus commissioned me to do. I went through the motions of it."[82]

What About When People That Don't Get Healed?

John Wimber saw many people healed of cancer in his ministry, yet he himself died of cancer. Billy Joe Daugherty, founding pastor of Victory Christians Center in Tulsa, Oklahoma, saw countless healings. He also passed away of cancer. Can I explain why one person gets healed and the other does not? No, I can't.

Fortunately, I don't have to.

I am not God, and I cannot heal anyone in my own strength. God heals, I don't. I can relax and pray for healing in such a way that no matter what happens, people will have experienced God's love through me. I get to see the sick healed when I work together with God and together we heal the sick.

For years I have coached my son and daughter's soccer team. One of my instructions was that if they were near the opponent's goal, they were to shoot. They did not score every time they shot, but they would never score if they never shot. It is the same with praying for the sick, prophesying, and sharing our faith with unbelievers—if we do not do it, people will never receive it.

The more we share our faith with people, the more people may believe in Christ. The more believers are praying for the sick, the more people will get healed. The more we prophesy, the more God can speak to people through us.

Keep praying for the sick, prophesying, and sharing your faith. Expect that healings, salvations, and miracles will take place. Whether people get healed, saved, or hear an accurate word from God or not, let them experience that you sincerely care for them. Praying for the sick, prophesying, and sharing the message of Jesus is one of the most loving things we can do.

Because, how can they hear unless we speak? How can they be healed unless we pray? "How, then, can they call on the one they have not believed in? And how can they believe in the one of whom they have not heard? And how can they hear without someone preaching to them? And how can anyone preach unless they are sent? As it is written: "How beautiful are the feet of those who bring good news!" (Romans 10:14 -15)

Healing the sick and speaking God's word is a normal part of sharing the message of Jesus.

Chapter 12
How to Grow in Power Evangelism

(Offering healing, words of insight, and more on the street in Amsterdam.)

"I will not venture to speak of anything except what Christ has accomplished through me in leading the Gentiles to obey God by what I have said and done---by the power of signs and wonders, through the power of the Spirit of God. So from Jerusalem all the way around to Illyricum, I have fully proclaimed the Gospel of Christ." --Apostle Paul, Rom. 15:18-19

"My message and my preaching were very plain. Rather than using clever and persuasive speeches, I relied only on the power of the Holy Spirit." 1 Cor. 2:4 (NLT)

What is Power Evangelism?

Power Evangelism is using prophecy, healing, deliverance, and the presence of God to share the Gospel with individuals.[83] The term was first made popular by the late John Wimber in his book that carried that title.[84]

In a culture that focuses on rational arguments for or against God, it is extremely helpful to be able to bypass people's minds and touch their hearts with the power of God through a healing or a word of knowledge. If we can get people to experience the power of God, they may be much more open to hearing more about Jesus. If believers experience the love and power of God, they may be less likely to walk away from God and the church.

I regularly see that people who want to hear nothing about Jesus suddenly are open to listening to me after they are healed or receive an accurate word of knowledge. The power of God released in signs, wonders, and miracles is the key to Power Evangelism. It is the same model established by Jesus and the apostles.

Jesus told us, *"Everything I can do, you can do better"* (John 14:12). The Apostle Paul took Him seriously. His primary strategy of doing evangelism and church planting was to go into an area and let the Holy Spirit use him to change lives. Paul healed the sick, raised the dead, prophesied, and got words of knowledge for people at every step in his missionary journeys. (Everything in this book is modeled after his ministry.) He did this from Jerusalem to Illyricum, and now that we have modern air travel, I believe we can share the Gospel all over the world using Paul's ministry methods.

The methods of Paul, (signs, miracles, and wonders) were the methods of Jesus, and using them ushers in the Kingdom of God. The same Holy Spirit that raised Jesus from the dead is now in us. He wants us to prophesy, heal the sick, raise the dead, cleanse the lepers, and freely give everything that has been freely given to us (see Matthew 10:7-8). Signs and wonders are to follow the preaching of His Word so that people know that He is *real*! Jesus Christ is our best example of a Power Evangelist.

How to Grow in Power Evangelism (PE)

Two great examples mentioned in the previous chapter of modern day power evangelists are Todd White and the late John Wimber. I too have experienced seasons in my life where I see hundreds of people get healed not only at churches, but on the street, on airplanes, at psychic fairs, and in offices. Growing in power evangelism is a lot of fun. However, not everyone will understand or appreciate it.

On an airplane flight, I sat next to a pastor from a mainline church who was dumbfounded as to why I pray for random strangers for healing. He literally asked me after I told him about Power Evangelism, "Why do you do that?"

It was outside his realm of experience or practice.

On the flight back however, the woman sitting next to me was dumbfounded when I told her I was a preacher. That did not make sense to her either. What did make sense was when I prayed for her in Jesus' name and all the pain in her back disappeared! She was so happy that when I spoke at a church in her hometown, she gladly brought her best friend to come hear me. God made an impression on her life, and the healing in her physical body opened her heart to hear His Word preached.

Everybody is looking for Jesus, but they do not know that it is Jesus whom they are looking for. Whenever I give a presentation at a psychic fair, I do not use any Christian terminology because some people are hostile to the Church and to Christianity. I simply title my lecture, "Demonstrations of the Supernatural Power of Love."

Everybody is looking for Jesus, but they do not know that it is Jesus whom they are looking for.

I then proceed to tell testimonies of when people have gotten healed by my *"source."* Then I tell everyone that my source is going to heal people. As soon as people begin getting healed, I then offer to reveal my source of healing power. I then reveal that Jesus Christ is the one who is healing people through me! At that point, I can share everything I want to about Jesus Christ and His message, because people have seen evidence of His healing power.

After sharing the Gospel, I will ask who would like to receive a personal word from Jesus Christ. Normally *everyone* present wants to receive a personal word. People are sometimes amazed and confused because they did not know that the Church and Jesus Christ has authority and spiritual power. This is a practical example of sharing the Gospel with signs and wonders and the power of the Holy Spirit.[85]

The first prostitute whom we could pray with to accept Christ did so after many months of me visiting and praying for her. She was so open because after one of my colleagues prayed for her, her chronic back pain disappeared completely.

Walking in the ministry and authority of the Holy Spirit is incredibly powerful when sharing the love and message of Jesus Christ. In a world that is so often closed to our words, the life-giving power of God will open hearts and change lives.

In *Miracle Work*, Jordan Seng shares his method for growing in power to do evangelism. Seng shares that when authority, gifting, faith, and consecration combine, they yield power. Let's look at each of these elements separately.

Authority

All authority comes from relationship. Spiritual authority comes from being close to Jesus. Jesus tells us to remain in Him and that *"If you remain in me and my words remain in you, ask whatever you wish, and it will be done for you"* (John 15:7).

Just like Jesus, our authority comes from doing what we see the Father doing and saying what we hear the Father saying (see John 5:19). My daughter cannot tell me what to do unless she is getting orders from her mother. When she is carrying out her Mama's orders, then she can make her Daddy jump quickly because she is speaking in the name of her Mama.

Shawn Bolz says that you can only have authority over people if you truly love and care about them. Like the Apostle Paul, we should strive to use our authority to build people up and love them as Christ loves us. It is of utmost importance that our authority be *relational.* The weakest form of authority is positional, when we tell people what we do because of our title or position. Authority that comes from our own example is far better. Then we can say "do what I do" or as Paul said, *"Follow me as I follow Christ"* (1 Corinthians 1:11).

Gifting

Paul admonishes us to eagerly desire spiritual gifts, especially prophecy (see 1 Cor. 14:1). I have grown in the gifts of healing and prophecy by studying them and seeking out individuals who have strong spiritual gifts. I ask God for these gifts myself and have seen Him grant me my request. It was after reading books from John Wimber and Gary Best that I began regularly getting words of knowledge, which led to healings. I believe these gifts are available for all believers.

I regularly minister with teams with individuals who have strong spiritual gifting I don't have (yet). When working together, everyone grows, and team ministry can be a lot more dynamic than alone. If you want to grow in giving out spiritual gifts, ask God for them and hang out with people who are further along than yourself. I look for people who are more experienced than I am, and I look for people who want to learn and grow from me. Gifting goes both ways. However, always look for those who use their gifts in love and relationship.

Faith

It is very scary to walk up to a complete stranger and offer to pray for their healing or to give an encouraging word for them. What are they going to say? Are they going to think I am crazy? Maybe they will, but maybe they will not. Maybe they will experience God.

Recently I went to downtown Amsterdam to share God's love and power on the street. The first thirty minutes, no one accepted my offer of prayer. That was until we saw a group of high school kids who were goofing around. As soon as the first student experienced healing in his knee, more of them started asking us to pray for them or tell them what we saw in them. In a manner of five minutes, we saw about five healings take place. We got to talk and pray for an entire group of students who thought they where just on a city field trip!

One of the fathers came to us afterwards and told us his son was healed and that we truly had awesome gifts. We got to share more about Jesus and got to pray for him and other students before they had to get on the bus and leave.

Faith requires action, because faith without works is dead. I don't want to just talk about healing or prophecy, I want to *do* it. This requires taking risks. As Wimber always said, *"Faith is spelled R-I-S-K."*

Faith requires action, because faith without works is dead.

Consecration

Spiritual disciplines such as fasting, prayer, and sacrificial giving are also great catalysts for growing in Power Evangelism. God's presence brings power with it.

Entire days of prayer and fasting where I spend hours prophesying over people definitely speeds up development and accuracy of spiritual gifts. If you don't see healings take place immediately, keep praying and believe that breakthrough will come. We do not *earn* spiritual power, but we do position ourselves to receive it from God.

Power Evangelism Growth Process

Here is a helpful chart to how the process of growing in PE may look like. [86]

Power Evangelism Growth Process

Identity Founded in Gospel	-The bedrock for practicing Power Evangelism -Everything feeds back into who you are in Christ.
Activation of Spiritual Gifts	-Basic Prayer Training Course or School of Prophecy (level 1)
Practice in Created Spaces	-Small Group -Holy Spirit Night
Practice Outside Created Spaces	-Prophetic words to people anywhere and anytime. -Healing people who have not asked for prayer.
Use your eyes outside of your church	-Start with healing conditions you can see. -Work your way up in RISK with conditions. -Ask for feedback and find out if they are healed.

Add Revelatory Component	-Start with words of knowledge for healing. -Prophesy over people as well.
Lean into Evangelism	-Power comes first, then evangelism.
Keep Adding Risk	-Groups of people. -Bolder claims of what Jesus will do.
Train Others	-Introduce people to process and walk them through it.

It is good to begin in a small private group instead of immediately trying it out in large public service. Some people keep a detailed journal of what they have tried and what has or has not worked. How many words have I given? How many were accurate? How many people have I prayed for healing? How many were healed? How many words of knowledge did I dare give? How many were right?

The Benefit of Practicing Power Evangelism in Public Places

Jesus literally said that we should go to the streets and bring people to know Him (see Luke 14:26). An important evangelistic encounter for Jesus occurred when He was thirsty and tired, sitting at a public well by a Samaritan village (see John 4). That encounter led to an entire village believing in Him. A divine encounter can be waiting for us at a restaurant or at the grocery store.

Though extremely daunting, practicing PE with strangers is good. It is good because they are strangers and you do not know anything about them and you may never see them again. This is a great way of meeting new people and learning how to share God's love and power in a way that people can understand. The more you do it, the more you learn.

In the Netherlands, I have learned that there are certain groups of people that are often more open to have a "spiritual" conversation. If people are walking fast to a shopping center, they most likely will not be interested in stopping to have a conversation. If they are sitting around at a park or public place doing nothing, they may be excellent candidates.

I have also experienced that older people often have prejudices against church and Jesus Christ so that they are often not as open for a conversation. I normally look for some young adults who are hanging out with whom I can talk with. Do not talk to everyone you see; instead, ask God to lead you to the right individuals. Some days, you may have a lot of conversations and other days few. It is like fishing, some days you have a lot of bites and other days few.

No matter how people may react, do not give up. The following testimony illustrates the importance of not giving up.[87]

> After a crash course in Power Evangelism with Matt in Belgium, a spark was ignited inside me to continue. Understanding in part how God could use me to prophesy and heal the sick, I wanted to spread the power of this incredible love with everyone.
>
> Returning home to England after the week in Belgium, I was so stirred up to continue what God had started to do through me. I decided to go for a walk around town, meet people, heal the sick, and prophesy. I was out for about an hour, and no one wanted to speak to me. I felt rejected. I stumbled over my words. I became so fearful to speak to anyone. In that next year, I only dared twice to give someone a prophetic word. I felt like a failure.
>
> The next year, I went to a town called Cwmbran in Wales. There I experienced God move in a powerful way. I went with other believers to a skate park where roughly thirty young

> people were skating. I tried to begin a conversation by asking if I could test out their scooters. I have no experience with scooters, so thankfully I did not fall. I began speaking to them about Jesus and sharing the Gospel. Many listened, but not for very long. They kept one ear on what I was saying as they continued to skate. After I finished talking, I told them that Jesus is alive today and loves to show people how much He loves them. One way is through healing. Then I asked, "Do any of you have any pain?"
>
> I guess being in a skate park, they all had a reason to raise their hands. I commanded one ankle to be healed in the name of Jesus and the young boy was healed instantly. He and his friends very surprised at the healing. (I was also a little surprised.)
>
> They all wanted Jesus to heal them also, and He did! Around ten young people — everyone I prayed for — were healed. They all experienced the power of God. At the end, I asked if the wanted to accept Jesus into their lives as Lord and Saviour, and eight of them prayed to accept Jesus.
>
> In the last three years, God has stretched me, and I have grown in PE. I am amazed each time when Jesus heals someone or *speaks into someone's life through me.*

Evangelism, like prophecy, is simple. Your job is not to argue with people but to show them God's love and power in order to share the truth. The more you do it, the better you get at it. However, it is important to do it with the right attitude. We do not want to come across as used car salesmen when we present Jesus; we want to act and speak just like He does. The motivation behind doing Power Evangelism is just as important (or even more important) than doing Power Evangelism. These values reflect Jesus. Here are some core values of power evangelism.

Core Values

Core Values of PE = Love, Humility, Peace, Honor, Power, Joy, & Nike[88]

Love

Jesus said that there will be people who have prophesied, healed the sick, and cast out demons...but who do not know Him (see Matt. 7:20-23). Our main goal in PE is to love people the way God loves us using His supernatural power.

Our main goal in PE is to love people the way God loves us using His supernatural power.

Paul says to follow the way of love and eagerly desire spiritual gifts (see 1 Cor. 14:1). It is not an accident that 1 Corinthians 13, the love chapter, is placed in between chapters 12 and 14, which are all about spiritual gifts. If we do not love, we are not reflecting God because He is love.

Humility

I define humility as simply power under the control of love. I have and continue to make mistakes whenever I operate out of insecurity and pride. Jesus and Moses were incredibly humble men, and so I believe prophetic people must follow their examples.

Whenever ministering at another church or ministry, I always place myself under the authority of the leader of that place. I come to serve and build the church up, and humility is an important element for this to take place. Don't aim at winning arguments, but winning *hearts*. This means we don't have to have the final word, and we don't have to strive but be at peace. God's power works best when we are at peace.

Peace

The power of God works best when we are at peace and at rest. I function best when I am not trying to force something to take place, but remaining in God's peace. When stepping out, it is helpful to remain relaxed. People don't care what you know until they know you care, so find ways to connect to people in a sincere and not pushy manner. Try to avoid coming across as a used car salesman. Continue a conversation with people as long as they are engaged. Power works best when we are at peace.

People don't care what you know until they know you care.

Honor

"True prophetic ministry is looking for gold in the midst of the dirt in people's lives."[89] Whenever speaking in the name of God, we desire to show people how valuable they are and how much He loves them. Our goal is to honor and love people with the same love and honor that God gives us. Add and don't take away value to people.

Power Through God's Presence

All our supernatural power is present because of the presence of God. Where God is, darkness, fear, depression, and sickness flees. The kingdom of God is not just words but power (see 1 Cor. 4:20). Our main job is to get people to connect to the presence of God. When people experience God, everything changes. This is why living a lifestyle of being connected to God can naturally lead to the supernatural taking place in our lives.

Joy

Loving God and loving people is fun! His kingdom is not about rules but righteousness, joy, and peace in the Holy Spirit (see Rom. 14:17). Friends have told me how relaxed and fun doing Power

Evangelism with me can be. I am not out to win arguments or force people to believe something; I get to help people experience Jesus. It can seriously be a lot of fun.

Nike- "Just Do It!"

A young man at a Bible School told me he had never seen anyone healed through his prayer. Immediately I said, "Well, let's go do it."

We found someone in the building with a headache whose pain left after he prayed for him. As a church, we are often over-taught and under-challenged. Don't just read about Power Evangelism—go do it.

Step out full of love, humility, and the power of God to love people by offering to pray for their healing. Ask God to give you words of wisdom and knowledge for those around you. Then expect healings and revelation to begin taking place sooner or later.

During one of the first youth conferences I did in Eastern Europe, a leader asked me, "Why aren't there healings in my country?" That weekend four people were healed when he prayed for them! More importantly, he has become a key leader who has inspired other people to do the same thing.

Thanks to him and people like him, hundreds of people in their city are regularly being prayed for and getting healed on the streets and in public places. They were not content simply talking about Power Evangelism, they decided to do it.

Are you ready for Power Evangelism, using prophecy, healing, deliverance, and the presence of God to share the Gospel with individuals? Take the love and authority Jesus has given you, the gifts of the Holy Spirit, and position yourself to receive power to share God's message of hope to the ends of the earth.

Cultivate the values of love, humility, peace, honor, power, joy and Nike. Just do it!

Conclusion: Prophesy, Heal the Sick and Do "The Stuff"

"You mean I gave up drugs for *that*?" –John Wimber

"The seed that fell among thorns stands for those who hear, but as they go on their way they are choked by life's worries, riches and pleasures, and they do not mature". (Luke 8:14, NLT)

What is your dream? What is your passion? Do you want to prophesy, heal the sick, get words of knowledge, and lead people to Jesus? What steps are you taking to make that a reality?

Often, we are over-taught and under-challenged to do what God has inspired us to do. Let me challenge you now. Are you going to put this book on the shelf and forget what you have just read, or are you going to do something about it?

A friend of mine, Juriaan Beek, has seen many people get healed on the streets in the Netherlands. His strategy of cultivating and developing this ministry was very simple. Every week he decided that he was going to go out and pray for people and not worry about whether people were going to be healed or not. The more he stepped out, the more healings and miracles took place. One of the experiences that really helped change his life was when he saw a paralyzed woman healed while he was ministering at a psychic fair.[90] Experiencing the power of God changes you forever.

Many times, when I go practice praying for the sick or giving words of encouragement on the streets, people think I am crazy. Yet, I have seen people's lives changed by taking radical steps of faith. If my fear of people's "NO's" paralyze me, then I will not get to experience the healings, signs, and wonders that might take place when people say YES. When people say, "Yes," anything is possible.

"It is not because things are difficult that we do not dare,
it is because we do not dare that things are difficult. -Seneca[91]

Do The "Stuff"

In 1963, John Wimber was a "beer guzzling, drug abusing pop musician, who was converted at the age of 29 while chain-smoking his way through a Quaker-led Bible study." He was fascinated by the supernatural healings, signs, and wonders of Jesus.

After going to weeks of boring church services, he went to a church leader and asked, "When do we get to do the stuff?"

"What stuff?" the leader replied.

"You know, the stuff here in the book. The stuff Jesus did, like healing the sick, raising the dead, healing the blind—stuff like that."

He was told that those things didn't happen anymore, to which John replied, "You mean I gave up drugs for *that*?" [92]

Wimber believed what Jesus said and taught was to be *done* (see Luke 9:1-2; 10:1-3; Matt. 28:18-20). He was not content to only have an intellectual faith, but desired to experience God as well. A dangerous addiction for Bible-believing Christians is living for comfort and for the approval of men. Comfort and fear of men can choke out a dynamic faith.

Comfort and fear of men can choke out a dynamic faith.

An ancient proverb tells of a man whom we will call Harry. He had received a special gift from the gods. It was a little nutshell with a red cord which had very special powers. Whenever Harry had a problem, all he had to do was pull the red cord and the problem would go away. For example, if he had a test on Friday, he would pull the red cord on

Thursday and it would be Saturday. He had passed the test. Harry was so happy with his shell and the little red cord that he always kept it with him.

A difficult discussion with his boss, wife, or kids was to be solved by pulling on the little red cord. This little red cord was his secret to success and happiness. With it, he achieved the western dream of owning a house, two cars, 2.5 kids, and a dog.

However, Harry never saw his children's birth or wondered if he could make a mortgage payment. The little red cord took care of all his fears and discomfort. He had a wonderful vacation home and was very much liked at his work. He had a comfortable life, and everyone thought he had it all together. He had become a slave to being comfortable.

Harry's addiction to the red cord allowed him to maintain an illusion of having everything under control. No one needed to know his secret, and no one needed to get too close to him because he had a safe solution for everything. Harry loved his feeling of safety. He liked seeing his kids grow up and succeed in school. When his children had relational problems or when they needed him to be around, he would pull on the string and everything would be solved. What an ideal life…right?

Wrong!

When Harry turned ninety and his wife had passed away, he looked back and realized he had never really *lived.* Because he had always chosen the "safe" route, he had never experienced real pain, difficulty, joy, peace, or the delight of a great victory. Harry lived in a "safe mode" of life and never took any risks. He always played it safe. Now that his life was nearly over, he was full of regrets. What a tragedy.

Taking risks means I refuse to be a slave to *comfort*. I will not pull on the red cord and avoid difficulties and problems. We only get to live life once. There is no dress rehearsal.

Do you dare to throw away any red cords in your life and start living today? What is keeping you from turning off the "safe mode" of life and doing that which God made you to do?

A reoccurring vision I had in 2010 was of me walking up to a willow tree and pulling on its branches. As I did that, oil appeared on my hands. I interpreted this vision as me placing a demand on the anointing or gifting of believers who have gone before me such as: Oral Roberts, John Wimber, John Wesley, Paul, Peter, Abraham, Elijah, and, of course, Jesus Christ Himself.

When praying, I would imagine a bucket full of water above me. Every time I prayed, I would pull down more water upon myself. It is an image of praying that God's kingdom come and His will be done on earth as it is in heaven. I don't want to pull a red cord for comfort; I want to pull heaven down to earth.

As time progressed, I reimagined the willow tree, but this time with myself sitting in the tree. My desire is to become a source of inspiration, instruction, and activation so that others can learn how to do the same kind of things Jesus did—and even greater.

Paul longed to see the believers in Rome so that he could impart spiritual gifts into their lives (see Romans 1:11). Paul admonished Timothy not to neglect the spiritual gift that was given to him through prophecy when the elders laid hands on him (see 1 Timothy 4:14). Wimber once said that the Church tends to inspire and educate people, but not equip them.[93] I pray that this book will help not only inspire and educate you, but activate and equip you as well.

In 2010, after hanging out with Prophet Bruce Foster in Chicago, the prophetic exploded in my life. He answered my question regarding how to prophesy with the words, "The same Holy Spirit I have, you do too. Just do it!"

In that same year, after reading books from John Wimber and Gary Best from the Vineyard movement, similar kinds of miracles and healings began taking place in my life as the ones that I read about. Phil Strout, the current leader of that movement, also laid his hands on me and blessed me. That year the prophetic and healing ministry exploded in my life. I have written this book so that perhaps what has happened in my life; can also develop in yours. Kind of like the following message someone sent to me on Facebook.

> Hey Matt! I was thinking of you recently and even more than in the past years. You don't know this, but you've had a really big impact on me - especially in prophesying and healing the sick. It was about two or three years ago when we met. The lessons you taught and the words God spoke into my life through you have really helped me to grow in the area of spiritual gifts and reaching out to the lost. I have seen so many people touched by the love of God through a healing or a word of knowledge. All glory to God who gives to all freely! I am thankful to have met you. Thank you for your faith and obedience to God.

I want to see another person equipped and released to prophesy, get words of knowledge, and heal the sick: *you*, the person reading this book.

Do you want to do the same kind of things Jesus did? Is Jesus Christ the Lord and Savior of every area of your life? Do you want to live a Christianity that is not just about talk, but of power? (see 1 Cor. 4:20)

If so, then let your faith be greater than your fear. Allow God's Spirit to fill your heart with His love so that you can love others in the same way that He loves us. Then step out by faith and Nike it—Just Do It!

Allow God's Spirit to fill your heart with His love so that you can love others in the same way that He loves us.

Just do "the stuff!"

"Heal the sick, raise the dead, cleanse those who have leprosy, drive out demons. Freely you have received; freely give" (Matthew 10:8).

"The same Holy Spirit I have...you do too! Just do it!"

Appendix A
Ministry Evaluation Form

This form is for everyone who has experience prophetic and/or healing ministry. This helps us to improve our teaching and continue to get feedback so we can grow in the prophetic and healing ministry. Please be honest and fill in what you would like to fill in.

What was the date and location of the ministry?

How did you experience it? Did you experience healing in your body? If so, explain.

If you experienced healing, do you have any doctor's papers that can confirm that the healing took place?

Was the ministry done in a way that encouraged, strengthened, and comforted you?

Did you experience God speaking to you through the prophetic ministry? If so, what percentage of the word do you feel was God speaking to you?

Were there significant traceable details or information given regarding your life? If so, feel free to share.

Is there anything else you would like to tell us concerning our time of ministry?

Thank you so much for your feedback. We are honored that we got to serve you. May we have your e-mail to further follow up on the prophetic words and/or healings you may have experienced during this time of ministry?

About the Author

Matthew Helland (M. Div., Oral Roberts University) has served for over a decade as a minister in Amsterdam, the Netherlands. He serves with his wife and four children. They have planted a church in Amsterdam and are now focusing on reaching out to prostitutes in that city's famous Red Light District.

He often travels to different nations to train individuals and churches in how to grow in prophecy and the gifts of the Holy Spirit. For more information or requests for training go to www.prophesyandheal.com.

Endnotes

[1] This was not an audible conversation, but one that took place inside of his heart.
[2] Foster, Richard. Prayer: *Finding the Heart's True Home.* London, Hodder and Stoughton, 2008, pg. 259.
[3] Foster, ibid, pg. 262.
[4] Putman, Putty. *School of Kingdom Ministry Manual.* Coaching Saints Publications: USA, 2013. pg 10.
[5] Tucker, Chene. *In Search of Purpose...Enroute to Destiny: Your Fourteen Week Appointment with God-Men's Manual. Tulsa: Polished Arrows International, 2004, pg. 47.*
[6] Keller, Timothy. *Preaching: Communicating Faith in an Age of Skepticism.* Penguin Random House: New York, 2015, pg. 1.
[7] https://thequietstreet.wordpress.com/2012/07/22/if-the-spirits-not-moving-ill-move-him/
[8] http://jeshilawokovu.blogspot.nl/2016/06/26-william-booth-quotes-and-50-william.html
[9]Hagin, Kenneth E. *How You Can Be Led by the Spirit of God.* Faith Library Publications:Tulsa, Ok, 2006, pg. 75.
[10] Hagin, Kenneth E. *ibid.* pg. ix.
[11] Hagin, ibid, 115.
[12] http://www.manta.com/c/mmygxhz/landers-window-exterior-cleaning-inc
[13] www.lomalux.com
[14] http://www.dwillard.org/articles/artview.asp?artID=43
[15] http://www.truenorthquest.com/george-washington-carver/
[16]http://www.bbc.co.uk/religion/religions/christianity/people/williamwilberforce_1.shtml
[17] Benge, Janet and Geoff. *Gladys Aylward.* YWAM Publishing: Seattle, 1998, pg. 19-30.
[18] Foster, Bruce taught this in May 2016 at our church in Amsterdam.
[19] Putman, Putty. *ibid,* pg 177.
[20] Henri Nouwen sermon is at https://www.youtube.com/watch?v=v8U4V4aaNWk
[21] https://meetingintheclouds.wordpress.com/2014/07/11/i-must-lose-in-order-to-gain/

[22] I gave this word of knowledge on the Deborah Sweeton Show. You can see this word of knowledge around minute 26.04 at https://vimeo.com/16952335
[23] Best, Gary, *Naturally Supernatural: God may be closer than you think.* Vineyard International: Cape Town Publishing, 2008. (Kindle location 805-808)
[24] Keller, Timothy. Humility. Sermon at http://www.gospelinlife.com/humility-6125
[25] St. Ignatius of Loyola. *Spiritual Exercises of St. Ignatius of Loyola.* translated by Father Elder Mullar, 1914, pg. 23-25. I also recommend Larry Warner's book *Journey with Jesus* for those who want to experience the Spiritual Exercises of Saint Ignatius. Intervarsity Press: Downer's Grove, 2010.
[26] Wimber, John. *Everyone Gets to Play.* Ampelon Publishing: Boise. 2008, pg. 125.
[27] *School of the Prophets*, Iglesia Crusaders de Chicago, Printed in Colombia, 2004 pg 17.
[28] Robert Morris' testimony See video https://www.youtube.com/watch?v=AVpjy_R62bU
[29] Bickle, Mike, *Growing in the Prophetic.* Eastbourne: Kingsway Publications, 1995, pg. 183-191.
[30] McClain, Michelle. *The Prophetic Advantage.* Charisma House: Lake Mary, 2012, pg. 50, 51.
[31] Valloton, Kris. *De Profeten School.* Arrowz: Haarlem, 2016, pg. 85.
[32] Hagin, Kenneth, ibid, 120.
[33] Hagin, ibid, pg. 92.
[34] Hagin, ibid, 87-88.
[35] To see a video of this testimony go to https://youtu.be/Qx_-j18ha-A
[36] Beacham, Doug. *Rediscovering the Role of the Apostles and Prophets.* Lifesprings Resources: Franklin Springs, 2004.
[37] Beacham also published a book on growing in the gifts of the Holy Spirit, *Plugged into God's Power.* Charisma House: Lake Mary, 2002.
[38] School of Prophets, ibid, pg. 26
[39] Cooke, Graham. *Developing Your Prophetic Gifting.* Kent: Sovereign World Ltd., 1994, pg. 199-201. I discovered this in Harrison, Diane. *The Power of Prophetic Teams.* Essence Publishing: Ontario, Canada. 2013, Kindle Locations 199-202.

---

[40] Leo, Eddy. U*sing the Gift of the Holy Spirit in Small Groups. Sermon given in Fortaleza, Brazil, 20/8/2013.*
[41] https://www.facebook.com/caminodevida.bolivia
[42] Boot, Lex. *Handboek christelijke meditatie: Vertrekpunten, wegen en vruchten.* (Uitgeverij Boekencentrum, Zoetermeer, 2004), 117-123.
[43] Eckhart, John. *God Still Speaks.* Charisma House: Charisma House, 2009, pg. 10.
[44] Hagin, ibid, 119.
[45] Wimber, John. ibid, pg 7.
[46] John Eckhardt's 2016 book *Prophetic Activation* has most of these exercises as well as 150 other prophetic exercises with variations.
[47] http://krisvallotton.com/your-prophetic-word-could-change-the-world/
[48] Bolz, Shawn. *Translating God.* Icreate: Glendale, 2015. pg. 162-169. Here is video about getting words of knowledge wrong https://www.youtube.com/watch?v=bNV3ZFN-e0k.
[49] Bolz, Shawn, ibid, 162.
[50] Brito, Abel told me this in my home on 23/5/2017 in Amsterdam.
[51] List is adapted from John Eckhardt's 2009 book *God Still Speaks*: Charisma House: Lake Mary, 2009, pg. 223-225.
[52] Pool, Jan. *Autoriteit: Wandelen in Gods kracht.* Arrowz: Haarlem, 2016, pg. 9.
[53] Hagin, ibid, 119.
[54] Randy Clark told this story at the There Is More Conference in Ede, Holland in September of 2016.
[55] This section comes from David Betts teaching notes during a 2010 New Wine Conference in Amsterdam and Putty Putman's Prayer Models Card http://schoolofkingdomministry.org.
[56] Kevin Dedmon's book *The Ultimate Treasure Hunt.* Destiny Image Publishers: Shippensberg, 2007. tells more about doing this kind of evangelism.
[57] Putty Putman's *School of Kingdom Ministry Prayer Training Card.*
[58] This section is almost completely from David Betts' notes
[59] My Father, Dean Helland, sent me this story in a personal e-mail on 10/04/2016.
[60] Tunstall, Frank G. *The Simultaneous Principle.* Lifespring Resources: Franklin Springs, 2005, pg. 9-11.

[61] Blackaby, Henry and Richard. *Experiencing God.* Nashville: B &H Publishing Group, 1990, pg. 32.
[62] http://nos.nl/nieuwsuur/artikel/2032376-burn-out-groeiend-probleem-onder-jonge-werknemers.html
[63]Bolz, Shawn, ibid, pg. 47.
[64] Illustrated video about John Ferrier is at https://vimeo.com/2129916
[65] Roberts, Bob jr. *The Multiplying Church (Grand Rapids: Zondervan), 2008, pg. 7.*
[66] https://www.cmaresources.org/article/ltg
[67] https://www.cmaresources.org/article/dna
[68] http://www.goodreads.com/quotes/1468095-i-simply-argue-that-the-cross-be-raised-again-at
[69] http://www.wholesomewords.org/missions/biostudd.html
[70] http://www.metroworldchild.org/about-us/bill-wilson
[71] Foster, Richard J. *Streams of Living Water.* (Harper One, New York, 2000), pg. 42-44.
[72] Phil Strout teaching this statement can be found at: https://vimeo.com/2129916
[73] Wimber, John. *Power Evangelism.* Harper Row: New York. 1986, pg. 11.
[74] http://www.charismamag.com/spirit/spiritual-growth/16827-7-lessons-t-l-osborn-taught-evangelist-daniel-king
[75] Adams, Moody. *The Titanic's Last Hero: A Startling True Story That Can Change Your Life Forever.* Ambassador International: Greenville, 2012, Chapter 1.
[76] www.newlifewest.nl
[77] The video of the healing is at https://www.youtube.com/watch?v=HaDJorFHoDk.
[78] Wimber, John. *ibid, pg. 42-44.*
[79] Todd White's testimony is at https://www.youtube.com/watch?v=6MEPiT9HbB0.
[80] Seng, Jordan. *Miracle Work: A Down-to-Earth Guide to Supernatural Ministries* (Kindle Locations 239-245). InterVarsity Press. Kindle Edition.
[81] Marlene Kleppes dramatized testimony https://www.youtube.com/watch?v=z4TN2uxS7DA.
[82] Wimber, John. *ibid,* 2008, pg. 173.
[83] Putman, Putty. *ibid,* 2013, p. 176.
[84] Wimber, John. *ibid,* 1986.

---

[86] Putman, ibid, 177.
[87] Testimony from Julien Conor.
[88] Putman, ibid, 180-182. (I based these on Putman's core values he expresses here)
[89] http://krisvallotton.com/your-prophetic-word-could-change-the-world/
[90] See this healing at https://www.youtube.com/watch?v=xDUymhJN44A&t=409s
[91] http://www.goodreads.com/quotes/731385-it-is-not-because-things-are-difficult-that-we-do
[92] Pickerell, Eric, *The Secular Mystic: Mysticism and the Future of Faith in the West.* (Masters Thesis from Vrije Universiteit in Amsterdam), August 2013, pg. 78.
[93] Wimber, John, ibid, 2008, 172.

Endorsements

"This comprehensive manual is the most practical and useful book I have read on the subject of ministering prophecy, healing and words of knowledge. It has been a joy to observe Matt's growth in ministry as he and Femke walk out the calling of God together. Matt's teaching has helped many who once thought prophecy and words of knowledge were "spooky" learn to value and flow in those gifts. I know this book will be a powerful tool in equipping and releasing many more joyful carriers of Kingdom ministry!
-Norman Wilke, Pastor of SpiritLife Church, Tulsa, OK, USA, www.myspiritlife.tv

"I know very few that are as diligent and bold as Matthew Helland. For nearly two decades I have admired his desire and constant push against the confines of status quo Christianity. Matthew pushes the boundaries into the frontier of spiritual fire. In this book, you will find theology that will stir you as well as very helpful insights and practical instruction. This work should be considered for individual or study groups who desire to unlock the power of God for their communities."
-David McLendon, Pastor of New Covenant Church, Statesboro, Georgia, USA www.snccontine.com

"Watching Matt and his prophetic team minister was like seeing well trained and equipped commandoes entering into the field of the enemy to rescue prisoners. They awakened and activated everyone for more of God's presence. Their prophetic ministry comforted, encouraged and sparked new faith in people's lives. They shared the message of God's kingdom not with words only, but also with His power and authority. This helped change our church and caused people to step out and share the message of Jesus with new love, power and vigor."
-Gabor Vinsze, Pastor of Living Water Church, Budapest, Hungary, www.eloige.hu

"Few modern seminary graduates are known for writing on topics like prophecy and deliverance. Matthew Helland has dared to write a book that is biblical, contemporary, practical and autobiographical. I am pleased to recommend it."
-Thomson Mathew, DMin, EdD, Professor and Former Dean, College of Theology & Ministry, Oral Roberts University, Tulsa, OK, USA
www.oru.edu

"This book is not designed to sit on the shelf, it is designed to coach zealous disciples of Christ. Living for God is experiential and we should expect the signs that scripture promises will follow believers. It is time for the Church to rise and practice the biblically sound principals taught in this book in order to change the world."
-Anthony Holmes, Pastor and Prophet of Church of the Living Water, Fresno, California, USA, www.colw.net

"Matthew Helland has been growing and living every millimeter of what he expresses! If you have this book in your hands, do not commit the mistake of simply skimming through it. Apply its words to your life and you will experience God's love and power in new ways."
-Moises Pichardo, Campus Pastor, Oklahoma City, Oklahoma, USA
www.victoryiglesia.tv

"Prophesy and Heal the Sick is a fresh and important word for the Kingdom and the Church. Matt Helland has taken a careful, intentional and anointed approach to encourage Christians in their understanding of the prophetic and the healing power of Christ. This is a book for every believer to read and enjoy."
-Randell O. Drake, Bishop of New Horizons Ministries, I.P.H.C., www.nhmiphc.com

CPSIA information can be obtained
at www.ICGtesting.com
Printed in the USA
LVOW08s0008060817
543779LV00002B/4/P